BEA[R]
ATTACKS
in CANADA

Erin McCloskey

Lone Pine Publishing

The Publisher: Lone Pine Publishing
10145 – 81 Avenue   1808 B Street NW, Suite 140
Edmonton, AB T6E 1W9 Canada   Auburn, WA, USA 98001

Website: www.lonepinepublishing.com

Library and Archives Canada Cataloguing in Publication

McCloskey, Erin, 1970–
  Bear attacks / Erin McCloskey.

Includes bibliographical references.
  ISBN-13: 978-1-55105-562-6
  ISBN-10: 1-55105-562-7

  1. Bears--Canada. 2. Bear attacks--Prevention. 3. Bear attacks--Canada.
I. Title.

QL737.C27N258 2008   599.78'0971   C2008-901643-2

Editorial Director : Nancy Foulds
Editorial: Volker Bodegom, Sheila Quinlan
Production Manager: Gene Longson
Book Design & Layout: Michael Cooke
Cover Design: Gerry Dotto

Track illustrations by Ian Sheldon; bear illustrations by Gary Ross.
Photo credits: Alberta Fish and Wildlife (BearSmart Campaign) 183, 187, 189;
Haul-All Equipment 185; J. Mark Higley (Hoopa Tribal Forestry) 25; National
Park Service 16, 27, 29, 80, 117; JupiterImages 23, 68, 73, 74, 77, 84, 87, 91, 97,
125, 127, 137, 142, 145, 193; Mitchell K. Taylor 141.

We acknowledge the financial support of the Government of Canada through
the Book Publishing Industry Development Program (BPIDP) for our publishing activities.

PC: P5

Disclaimer

This book is not a guide as to how to survive a bear attack but simply a compilation of information intended to be a reasonably comprehensive reference based on the best available current knowledge, and it should by no means be considered authoritative.

For additional information, please visit www.bearscience.com.

Dedication

For my brother, Travis, and our Waterton bear!

Acknowledgements

First I would like to acknowledge the people who, despite hardship or tragedy from bear attacks, still value the existence of wild bears in Canada. I hope I have portrayed the accounts of the victims with accuracy and respect.

I owe a great deal of research credit to the assistance of each of the provincial and territorial wildlife departments, with special thanks to certain individuals who put in extra time and effort in providing statistical information, namely Russell Stashko of Alberta Fish and Wildlife's Bear Smart Campaign for sharing information, photos and resources; also Mike Badry at the BC Ministry of Environment; Hélène Jolicoeur and Michel Hout at the Ministère des Ressources naturelles et de la Faune / Wildlife Protection Québec; Jolanta Kowalski at the Ontario Ministry of Natural Resources; Hank Hristienko and Darryl Hedman from Manitoba Conservation; Tony Nette at the Nova Scotia Department of Natural Resources; Chris Callahan from the Newfoundland Department of Natural Resources; Kevin Craig from the New Brunswick Department of Natural Resources; and Mathieu Dumond, Raymond Mercer Jr., Joel Rose, Steve Pinksen, Julie Ross and Ross Hotson from the Nunavut Department of Environment, with sincere thanks to Mitch Taylor, Lily Peacock and Markus Dyck for their attention to the polar bear text.

Thanks to S/Sgts Rob de Boersap and Tom Roy and several commanders of the BC RCMP, to Down Mathews and Polar Bear International, to Mark Higley with Hoopa Tribal Forestry, and to Andrew Derocher and the IUCN/SSC Polar Bear Specialist Group. And, for answering so many technical questions (both recently and years ago at Uni!), thank you to David Paetkau of Wildlife Genetics International.

At last, I thank Shane Kennedy and Nancy Foulds for giving me the opportunity to write this book, and thanks to Volker Bodegom, Sheila Quinlan and Michael Cooke for their excellent work.

Contents

Introduction

Knowledge is a person's greatest weapon against any danger. But knowing how to defend yourself against a bear attack is only one lesson in your studies—throughout the abundant literature and websites that discuss bear attacks and avoidance, the most emphasized point is to learn about the animal. Learn about bears, including where they roam, what they eat, how they socialize, how they communicate through body language and other natural history and behavioural information. No amount of bear spray or food caching will do as much to increase your level of safety in bear country as much as an awareness and understanding of bears. Somewhere between being naïvely ignorant of the dangers that bears pose and being terrified into believing that all bears are dangerous killers, there is a position from which increased awareness and understanding of bears will increase your safety and enjoyment when in areas inhabited by bears.

Canada is home to all three species of North American bear: black, grizzly and polar. The black bear, a truly North American bear, ranges south all the way to Mexico and is found on no other continent. The grizzly bear is a subspecies of the brown bear, which also inhabits Europe and Asia. The grizzly and the Kodiak of Kodiak Island, Alaska, are the only genetically identifiable subspecies of brown bear in North America. Largely extirpated from the lower continental United States, the grizzly still exists in substantial numbers in Alaska and western Canada. Finally, although the polar bear's distribution is circumpolar, 60 percent of the world's polar bears inhabit Canada's generous share of the Arctic.

Whenever a bear kills or seriously injures a human and is believed likely to re-offend, it is usually killed. Each province and territory reports dozens of bears each year that have become identified as "aggressive bears" or "nuisance bears." Nuisance bears are ones that frequently enter human territory such as yards or campgrounds, show up at close range to people without seeming wary or seek out human food sources. These bears are typically relocated or destroyed.

Consider the bears' perspective. How often do people commit these same trespasses against bears? Collectively, we humans criss-cross bear territory with roads, trails and rails and go about picking the fruit, berries and mushrooms on which bears sustain themselves. Sometimes we appear without warning, coming face-to-face with a bear by stumbling upon the animal minding its own business, dozing in a clearing or enjoying its own picnic in a berry patch. These encounters most often result in the bear voluntarily removing itself, but every once in a while, such an animal also gets the idea to destroy the offending "wildlife"—the person.

Bears that are destroyed in "defence of life or property" (known as DLPs) are greatly outnumbered by bears that die from hunting, being killed on roads and railways or becoming food conditioned, which often results in the animals in question being put down as potentially problematic to humans. In Canada, each of the three species of bear is under a hunting quota in some part of its range. The black bear, which is considered a fur-bearing game animal, is hunted by the hundreds in each province and territory in which it is found. The grizzly is sought by trophy hunters, although it is given a reprieve in

PLACES OF SIGNIFICANCE TO THIS BOOK

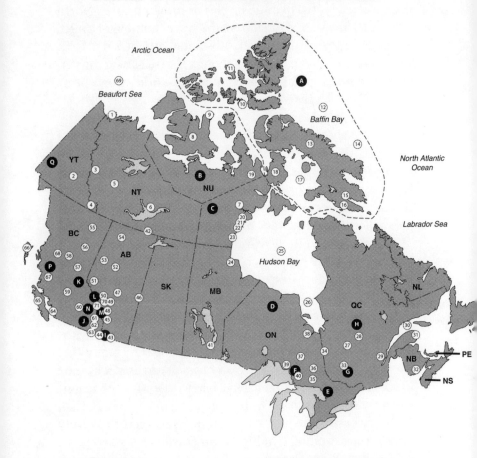

A	Baffin Region	I	Waterton National Park
B	Kitikmeot Region	J	Rosebery Provincial Park
C	Kivalliq Region	K	Bowron Lake (Bowron River)
D	Polar Bear Provincial Park	L	Jasper National Park
E	Algonquin Provincial Park	M	Banff National Park
F	Chapleau Crown Game Reserve	N	Mt Robson Provincial Park
G	La Vérendrye Wildlife Reserve	P	Tweeksmuir Provincial Park
H	Chibougamau Provincial Park	Q	Kluane National Park

Introduction

1	Kendall Island	26	James Bay	51	Grande Cache
2	Ross River	27	Lebel-sur	52	Swan Hills
3	Mackenzie Mnts	28	Waswanipi	53	Grande Prairie
4	Goz Lake	29	Valcartier		(Grovedale - about
5	Mackenzie River	30	St Lawrence		21km south)
6	Yellowknife	31	Gaspé	54	Zama Lake
7	Baker Lake	32	Hampton	55	Fort Nelson
8	Victoria Island	33	Lac Canimina	56	Fort St John
9	Stefansson Island	34	Abitibi Lake	57	Prince George
10	Resolute	35	Sudbury	58	Vanderhoof
11	Ellef Ringnes Island	36	Mattagami River	59	Williams Lake
12	Baffin Bay	37	Missinaibi River	60	Revelstoke
13	Baffin Island	38	Moose River	61	Radium Hotsprings
14	Davis Strait	39	Missinaibi Lake	62	Invermere
15	Iqaluit	40	Chapleau	63	Cranbrook
16	Kimmirut (Soper	41	Selkirk	64	Vancouver
	Lake)	42	Fort Smith	65	Vancouver Island
17	Foxe Basin	43	Castle River (near	66	Queen Charlotte Is
18	Melville Peninsula		town of Pincer Creek)	67	Bella Coola
19	Pelly Bay	44	Rocky Mountains	68	Burns Lake
20	Rankin Inlet	45	Calgary	69	Beaufort Sea
21	Corbett Inlet	46	Llyodminster	70	Sundre (northwest
22	Whale Cove	47	Edmonton		of Calgary)
23	Arviat	48	Canmore	71	Lake Louise (north
24	Churchill	49	Banff		of Banff)
25	Hudson Bay	50	Jasper		

various provinces and territories at various times (such as the three-year moratorium in Alberta that began in 2006). The hunting of polar bears in the Arctic is a cultural and economic mainstay.

Throughout history, humans and bears have typically been adversaries. Presumably, most bear hunters would agree that if they go stalking bears, they are putting their lives at risk, and that it is part of the price to pay in wanting to return to a somewhat natural, perhaps even primitive, calling. If the hunter misses the shot or becomes the hunted, it would not be hard to see it as an "eye-for-an-eye" situation. However, most people do not wish harm on bears, and of course nobody wants to be injured by a bear.

This book has two main objectives. The first is to foster public education and increase awareness of bears so that fewer people get hurt or die, fewer nuisance bears are created—humans are responsible for bears becoming nuisances—and fewer bears are killed, particularly females and cubs. The second objective is for people to recognize and understand two seemingly opposing facts. First, bear attacks are statistically rare when one considers the number of people and number of bears that cross each other's paths in Canada per day (which equates to many millions per year). Second, every bear is potentially dangerous, capable of attacking and may very well attack on any given occasion—therefore, one should never be overly complacent about the first fact.

UNDERSTANDING BEARS

Trying to understand a bear's primary motivations aids in understanding how the bear perceives and responds to human presence. These primary motivations are food, sex, raising young, investigating new stimuli and asserting dominance. They are not really so different from those of people, but we should never anthropomorphize—a bear is a wild animal, and, more importantly, each bear is unique and somewhat unpredictable. A bear that encounters a human is faced with the decision to avoid, investigate or attack, and this decision will have a positive or a negative outcome that will be learned and remembered. Studies on animal behaviour and intelligence have shown that of all carnivores, bears have the highest brain-to-body-mass ratio, that their behaviours are greatly influenced by remembered experiences and recalled outcomes of previous actions and that they pass these learned behaviours on to their offspring.

Within bear society, hierarchy is important. Females must be as assertive as males in order to protect their young; females with cubs that cannot deter a male may be slain by him. Males challenge each other for dominance over territory and mates. In these challenges, the bears usually employ restraint and avoidance through posturing, vocalizations and bluff charges rather than direct contact. However, a juvenile (subordinate) that challenges an older and stronger bear usually winds up severely injured or dead. Each of these categories—adult males, adult females with cubs and recently weaned or still-young juveniles—typically has very different motivations and behaviours that affect how they react to human presence.

Bears communicate through body language, posturing and personal space as well as through vocalizations such as growling, huffing, snorting and whining. Cubs make distress calls that resemble the crying of a human baby. A bear knows no threat or predator other than humans and other bears, so a person's posture, use of voice and treatment of the bear's space can affect how a bear responds or reacts, perhaps much like it would with another bear.

BEAR COUNTRY SAFETY TIPS

Before entering bear country, you must be prepared:
• research bear abundance and activities (what the bears are likely to be doing) in the place(s) you will be staying or travelling through
• learn about bear behaviour and habitat (for example, salmon-spawning streams invite high densities of fish-eating bears during spawning season)
• know how to identify and watch for signs of bears
• make sure that every member of your travelling group is familiar with the risks and avoidance techniques
• learn how to use bear spray or other technical deterrents (see Deterrents, p. 200) that you may choose to carry
• obtain basic wilderness first aid knowledge as well as a first aid kit before entering backcountry situations; check online or with continuing education departments for wilderness first aid courses (local camping supply stores, outdoor clubs and outfitters may be able to refer you to reputable local courses); a first aid kit should carry ample bandages, tourniquets, slings

and gauze as well as tape, butterfly stitches, antiseptic and antibacterial liquids or creams and painkillers
- because women may be at greater risk of bear attack while menstruating (the issue is still being debated), women may wish to take this factor into account when planning a trip; tampons are recommended over external pads
- tell authorities and family or friends your itinerary at the start your trip
- carry and know how to use emergency communication equipment such as satellite phones (for remote areas—they can be rented before your trip), and obtain and carry with you emergency phone numbers
- when travelling into isolated areas, carry a Personal Locator Beacon (PLB) and register it with the Canadian Personal Emergency Beacon Registry (http://beacons.nss.gc.ca/); in case of a serious emergency, with a push of a button it can relay your location coordinates to rescue personnel
- carry a Global Positioning System (GPS) receiver so that you have precise location coordinates to provide to emergency response personnel
- bring extra batteries for your communication and GPS equipment and keep the batteries warm—batteries do not last long in cold weather; for vehicles, consider thermal or low-temperature batteries such as VRLA-AGM lead-acid batteries (good to -30° C); regular (or even premium) alkaline and NiMH batteries do not last long at frigid temperatures, so (as of this writing) a better choice would be NiCads (if you have a suitable charger for use en route) or lithium (although more expensive).

IN THIS BOOK

Avoidance and safety recommendations in this book are a compilation of various sources, including government, scientific and lay people who work, live or play in bear country. This book is not a guide as to how to survive a bear attack but simply a compilation of information intended to be a reasonably comprehensive reference based on the best available current knowledge, and it should by no means be considered authoritative. However, it is intended to be useful.

To know how to avoid an encounter or to deal with one should it arise, it is important to know the basic biology and behaviours of bears. Each of the three species is presented in its own chapter with the following information:

- basic identification
- where in Canada the bear is found
- what densities and populations it has throughout Canada
- what habitat types it uses
- what time of year the bear uses certain habitat zones
- what the bear eats and how to recognize these food sources
- when the bear enters winter dormancy ("hibernates") and how to recognize its den
- when the bear comes out of winter dormancy, hungry and perhaps with new cubs
- what the common behaviours of the bear are and how to avoid being perceived as a threat
- what warning signals indicate that a bear intends to attack, bluff charge or act offensively
- what types of attack—predatory, offensive or defensive—are likely and how to react accordingly (*Note:* an encounter is not considered an attack until the bear physically contacts a person)

Following the three chapters on the three bear species are chapters on avoidance techniques and deterrents for when people are in areas where any of these bears may range. When living in, working in or visiting these areas, it is important to understand the risk of encountering bears and how to avoid a dangerous situation, or how to safely get out of a dangerous situation should you find yourself in one. When encounters do occur, it is important to know how to react and also how to protect yourself, so suggestions are offered as to how to deal with emergency situations.

Turn to the back of the book for information regarding plants that are attractive to bears (see Plant Index, p. 220). By recognizing the plants, you can be more aware of areas where you can expect to find bears feeding, and you can avoid camping near food sources that bears may want to defend against intruders.

To help ensure the safety of other people in the area, report all bear sightings and incidents to the park authorities or the local RCMP or conservation office (see the list of provincial phone numbers on p. 215).

Although no premature loss of human life is acceptable, injury and death are inherent risks for people living in or visiting bear country. Of the many Canadians who have lost loved ones or who have themselves been severely maimed by bears, very few indeed would want to see bears eliminated from Canada's wild places. As mighty symbols of wilderness, bears are truly part of Canada's cultural identity.

Black Bear

Ursus americanus
Kermode bear, cinnamon bear, glacier bear
ours noir in French, *sah dezo* in Dogrib, *sa dezene* in
K'áshogot'ine–Sahtúgot'ine–Shihgot'ine (North
Slavey), *shoh* in Gwich'in

The black bear is the most populous bear species in Canada and the most tolerant of human presence; thus it is the bear that people most frequently encounter. Statistically, this bear is less likely than either a grizzly or a polar bear to inflict harm on a human. For example, in British Columbia and Alberta, the number of human fatalities caused by black bears is about equal to the number caused by grizzly bears, even though black bears are about 10 times more plentiful in the region. The number of cases in this region involving serous injuries by black bears is only a fraction of the number caused by grizzlies.

Typically, an encounter with a black bear results in the bear fleeing, but habituated bears may simply ignore human presence. Problem black bears are almost always overly habituated to human presence, food stressed or food conditioned to human food sources—or a combination of the three. When natural cycles in productivity diminish wild food sources essential to bears, there is a higher rate of human-bear conflict. In addition, increased development in bear country reduces the bears' ability to find sufficient food or attracts them to human food sources. On rare occasions, black bears consider humans to be prey.

Human fatalities caused by black bears have occurred in most provinces and territories where black bears range; to date, in the Yukon and part of the Maritimes there have been no such incidents. In the western United States, black bear attacks are so rare that many people think of bears as harmless, Disney-like creatures of the forest. Abundant examples exist of black bears tolerating extremely imprudent actions by people—approaching very close to bears to photograph them, feeding them or taunting them with food and even throwing objects at them or chasing them—without causing these people any harm. Indeed, black bears are the most timid and least aggressive of the three bear species in Canada, and statistically they are a very low risk to human safety. However, serious injuries and fatalities have been caused by black bears, so any and every bear should be regarded with caution and respect.

BASIC IDENTIFICATION

Height to shoulder: 60–110 cm (2–3½ ft)

Total length: *male:* 1.3–1.9 m (4¼–6¼ ft); *female:* 1.2–1.6 m (4–5¼ ft)

Tail length: 8.5–18 cm (3¼–7 in), but well hidden in fur

Weight: *male:* 60–400 kg (130–880 lb), avg. 135 kg (300 lb); *female:* 40–235 kg (90–520 lb), avg. 70 kg (150 lb)

Fore paw: 10–16 cm (4–6¼ in) long; 9.5–14 cm (3¾–5½ in) wide; short claws make little or no imprint in track

Hind paw: 15–18 cm (6–7 in) long; 9–14 cm (3½–5½ in) wide; short claws make little or no imprint in track

Stride: 43–58 cm (17–23 in)

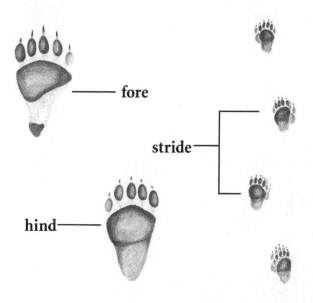

The male is generally 20 percent larger than the female; coastal populations are up to 50 percent larger than inland populations because of the high-protein salmon diet; northern inland populations are the smallest because of the short foraging season.

The name "black" bear is often a misnomer; the long, shaggy fur can be shades of brown, cinnamon, honey, pale blond and, rarely, albino white instead of black. Several interesting populations of black bear in Canada demonstrate these colour morphs in higher frequencies. Colour differences generally result from genetic drift in populations isolated on islands or separated by mountain ranges or by human encroachment fragmenting the habitat. Separate populations are often categorized as separate subspecies. Although certain colours predominate in a given subspecies, colour alone cannot be relied on to identify the subspecies.

The glacier bear (*U. a. emmonsii*) that occurs in the extreme northwest of BC is known for its often bluish colour. The Kermode (*U. a. kermodei*) or "spirit bear" of the northwest coast is popularly identified as white, but it can also be black, brown, light and dark auburn, bright yellow, golden, blue grey or a dark-and-light "pinto." Indeed, a white Kermode can have black offspring.

It is common for bears to be misidentified based on colour, particularly in the case of brown-phase black bears, which account for a significant fraction of grizzly bear stories. Light colour morphs are more frequent in western Canada (30 percent of black bears in the Yukon are brown in coloration), whereas the eastern black bear almost always has the typical glossy black fur with a tan muzzle, often with a white "V" or blaze on the chest.

The diagnostics of the black bear's physiology—the main features that distinguish it from the grizzly bear—are the straight snout and face in profile, prominent pointed ears, no shoulder hump and short black claws on the fore paws. When a black bear stands on its hind legs, the body profile slopes forward from the top of the hip. The legs are short and powerful, the body is short and stout, and the tail is very short and quite hidden in the long fur.

WHERE CAN YOU EXPECT TO ENCOUNTER A BLACK BEAR?

Black bears are found only in North America and range from the arctic treeline south to Florida and northern Mexico. The Newfoundland black bear population is thought to have been isolated since the end of the last glaciation; otherwise, black bears are found in a continuous distribution from west to east—from coastal British Columbia, including islands, across all of the Canadian provinces to the Maritimes, absent only from Prince Edward Island. Black bears range north into the three territories as far as the treeline.

Because of a lack of a coordinated and intensive effort from each province and territory to accurately determine the black bear population, the total black bear population in Canada is a gross estimation. Population counts are difficult and costly, and these forest dwellers are usually hidden from the view of airborne surveys. Therefore, although the national black bear population is often estimated at 500,000, there is

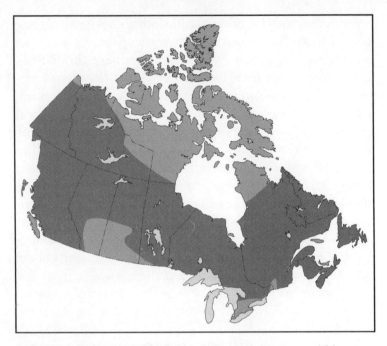

a very high degree of error, and the real figure could be anywhere in the range of 300,000–700,000.

For their homes and recreational activities, people often choose the same areas that the black bear inhabits—river valleys and forested areas, for example. This tendency to favour the same places, combined with the bear's high tolerance for human presence, makes for frequent encounters. The black bear is primarily a forest dweller, particularly large mixed forests with a large variety of tree and shrub species that provide nuts, fruits and seeds, and it is well adapted to climbing trees. Aspen, white spruce and black spruce trees are common representatives of black bear forest habitat.

This bear is also found in swampy areas near forests or shrub thickets, where it finds tender aquatic plants to eat. It prefers areas that combine forest (which provides seclusion and safety, especially with large trees to climb in order to flee danger) with open spaces and river valleys that provide berries, shrubs and grasses for food and streams for water. In the absence of grizzly bears, the black bear enters forest clearings and roadsides, south-facing subalpine meadows and disturbed places (such as burned areas) to graze on vegetation.

The black bear avoids grasslands and deserts, so it is not found in southeastern Alberta or southern Saskatchewan. In Manitoba, density estimates range from 0.65 bears per km^2 in the boreal forest to over 2.6 bears per km^2 in Riding Mountain National Park and Duck Mountain Provincial Forest (0.25 to over 1 bear per mi^2). Since the early 1900s, black bears have been re-occupying abandoned agricultural regions of the south and southwest. Found throughout most of rural Ontario, the black bear lives in higher densities along the southern edge of the Canadian Shield, where abandoned agricultural and previously deforested lands are seeing a southward expansion of black bear range. This range continues throughout Québec and the Maritimes (except Prince Edward Island).

In the extremes of its northern range in the Northwest Territories, the black bear is occasionally sighted on the tundra and in the Mackenzie Mountains, although it generally prefers river valleys, namely the Slave, Mackenzie and Liard rivers. In the Yukon, this species of bear is thinly distributed from the BC–Yukon border to the northern treeline near Old Crow; it is most numerous in the southern and central parts of the territory and in mountainous areas.

Black bear populations and densities are higher in wet climatic zones, where vegetation is more plentiful, than in dry regions. In coastal areas, where salmon spawning grounds provide additional food, black bear populations are at their densest, and humans near favoured food sources makes encounters with this animal more likely. British Columbia has the highest black bear population in the country, with densities in favourable habitats averaging one bear per 3 km^2 (1.1 mi^2).

Core home ranges (where the animals go about most of their day-to-day activities) for black bears are on average 13–40 km^2 (5–15 mi^2), although individual males have been observed ranging over areas of approximately 150 km^2 (60 mi^2). In the Northwest Territories, black bears probably have ranges 75–200 km^2 (30–75 mi^2), and far-ranging individuals have been observed over areas up to 320 km^2 (125 mi^2). Females have smaller ranges, from as small as 2 km^2 (0.8 mi^2) to as great as 117 km^2 (45 mi^2), with 5–25 km^2 (2–10 mi^2) being typical. The ranges of females are usually half the size of the males' ranges, and they may overlap with those of other, often related females, such as a sister or daughter.

Males compete with other males for dominance that gives access to as many females as possible. They do not tolerate another male's proximity and will fight to determine or defend hierarchy. Ranges are arbitrary and flexible, however, because during breeding season, some males may roam far in search of a mate. Through scent, scat, carrion or scratching on trees, males are highly aware of other bears in the vicinity, so they can choose to just give each other a wide berth. As a male bear gets older, larger and stronger, he begins to assert his dominance and begins to fight and chase off other males he encounters. If a young male bear does not avoid the established bear that it knows to be in the area and retreat, he must be willing to fight for dominance.

Black bears are normally seen throughout the year except in winter, when they prefer to slumber (see When Are Black Bears in Their Dens?, p. 26). They tend to be most active at dawn and dusk, unless they are food-conditioned to human food sources or garbage, in which case they may become distinctly diurnal (on roadsides) or nocturnal (in campgrounds).

The chance of encountering black bears varies with their seasonal behavioural and movement patterns. Spring and summer have the highest rates of encounters. The peak of breeding season in midsummer sees adult male bears most active and roaming throughout the greatest expanses of their range. Adult females will also be expanding their ranges during summer, particularly if they are weaning cubs, which they do in late spring and early summer. Mother bears allow female offspring to establish home ranges that overlap with their own, but male offspring will be forced to move outside their mother's range. Thus, young males need to travel up to 200 km (125 mi) to establish their ranges, and they have to avoid or be willing to compete with older, established bears. It is these younger, inexperienced and exploratory males that most frequently encounter human habitations and development.

WHAT DO BLACK BEARS EAT?

Black bears are classified as carnivores, but they consume less meat than vegetation, which can constitute up to 95 percent of the diet. In reality they are omnivores, eating almost anything with caloric value.

Black bears happily feed on berries such as raspberries, blueberries, soapberries (buffalo berries, soopolallie), strawberries, cranberries, crowberries, bearberries, elderberries and saskatoons (see Plant Index, p. 220). Berries offer higher energy and nutritional value than other plant food sources.

Bears work their way through the various berry species as they ripen throughout summer and fall. These berry patches are important to watch for when hiking, camping or working in bear country. Overwintered bearberries are an important food source for hungry bears just out of winter dormancy in spring—these berries have higher nutritional and caloric value than fresh bearberries in fall because their sugar content increases by two to three times over winter. Soapberries are widespread in open forests and in forest openings. The various blueberry species ripen from summer to fall, and they are found in a range of habitats from bogs to coniferous forests and alpine tundra. Many berry species, such as blueberry, grow as successional plants after forest fires but rarely after clearcuts because reforestation programs typically uses herbicides. Selective cutting and avoidance of herbicides improves bear habitat.

Trees with ripe fruits or nuts, whether domestic or wild, attract black bears. Black cherries and apples are especially enticing, as are acorns, hazelnuts, mountain-ash berries, hawthorn berries and beechnuts. Watch tree trunks for fresh scratch marks caused by climbing; if you see any, carefully look up the tree to see if the bear is still present. In spring, when many other foods are unavailable, black bears often eat the cambium layer of tree bark—the chew marks on trees are important signs to watch for that indicate bear presence. Also look for other plants of which black bears are particularly fond, such as horsetails, skunk cabbage and the catkins of willows and cottonwoods, all of which grow in forest openings, marshes and riparian areas in spring and early summer. These bears will eat fresh catkins, cones, shoots and leaves of woody plants such as conifers, aspen and birch. Dandelions and other wildflowers, clovers, grasses, forbs and sedges offer good grazing in spring and in disturbed sites, such as along roads and freeways, burned areas and avalanche chutes.

Most of the protein consumed by black bears comes from insects such as grasshoppers and colonial species of ants, bees

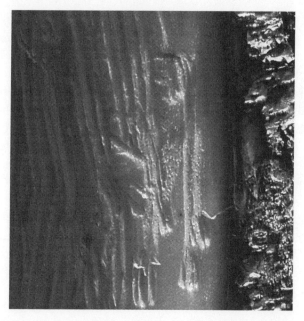

and wasps and their larvae. True to popular lore, black bears are especially fond of beehives (including those at bee farms); they eat both the honey and the bees. Other insects, such as dragonflies, can be regionally important. The meat in a black bear's diet sometimes comes from small mammals, such as rodents, or, rarely, calves of deer, moose, elk or caribou. Mammal carrion is a very important protein source for this bear as well as for grizzly and polar bears. Coastal bears thrive on salmon during their spawning runs, whereas inland bears may fish for pike, trout, walleye and suckers in streams and along the shallow margins of lakes. They also rob eggs from nesting waterfowl.

For northern bears that must survive with a narrow variety of foods and a short foraging season, berry crops are critical. When berry crops fail, as they do every few years, black bears are forced to travel widely in search of food; they can range up to 100 km (60 mi) to find new sources. Stressed bears can be more determined in their search for food, and their desperation can bring them into greater contact with people.

In all parts of the country, if natural foods are not easily available, black bears are quick to explore human-related food sources, primarily human garbage. Unsecured garbage dumps, which offer a concentration of readily available food, and improperly stored household garbage attract bears. Pet food that has been left outdoors, bird feeders, barbecues with food debris on the grills and rotting compost can also attract black bears to rural and suburban yards. Agricultural areas have to contend with black bears that raid corn and other grain crops and sometimes prey upon young lambs and calves.

Once black bears locate a non-natural food source, they return again and again—over a period of several days, weeks, months or even years—and they learn to associate human homes and campsites with food. In such cases, bears may even become destructive or dangerous; bears are often destroyed because they have become a "nuisance" or are perceived to be a threat to human safety. Live trapping and relocation can be a successful alternative to killing, but black bears have been known to return to a site after they have been transported as far as 80 km (50 mi) away.

WHEN ARE BLACK BEARS IN THEIR DENS?

In areas subject to accumulating snowfall, prolonged frigid temperatures and scarce food resources, black bears retire to their winter dens until conditions improve. They enter their dens by mid-October to early November and remain in them for about 3 months in the warmest areas and up to 7 months in the coldest areas. The den may be in a rock pile, a hole dug in the ground or a cave, or it may be in a hollow tree or beneath a fallen log or the roots of a fallen tree, under a large-diameter tree or in a snag, log or stump. A black bear den can be up to 25 m (80 ft) above the ground. These bears have even been found overwintering in haystacks. Many people do not consider black bears to be true hibernators because they can be roused from their slumber by warm weather or a disturbance and may be found briefly outside their dens, and their body temperature drops only a little during their winter dormancy.

Both male and female black bears den throughout the cold and food-scarce months. As a result, winter black bear encounters are rare, and the animals are not in hunting or feeding mode. Avoid disturbing a slumbering bear, though, because it may not appreciate your proximity or being woken.

Particularly when pregnant or with cubs, females den longer than the males. Black bears mate in spring, but embryo implantation is delayed until fall, around November. A female breeds only if she is without cubs. Northern black bears have a low rate of reproduction. Northern females reproduce only every 2–4 years, not breeding for the first time until 7–9 years of age, as compared to southern female bears, which first breed at 3–4 years. As a result, a female bear in the Yukon or Northwest Territories may only produce 2–4 litters in her 20-year lifespan.

A pregnant female delivers 1–4 (usually 2–3) cubs in winter (January or February) in her den. The tiny (250–400 g or 9–14 oz), hairless, blind cubs nurse while the female slumbers through winter. By April, the cubs are 15–20 cm (6–8 in) long and weigh 2–5 kg (4.5–11 lb), and the mother and cubs begin venturing outside the den. The cubs stay with their mother until their second summer and are weaned at 16–17 months. Cubs orphaned in their first summer have only a 30-percent survival rate.

When bears of both sexes emerge from their dens, they are hungry, and the mating season is around the corner (June). During the dormant winter fasting period, a female loses 20–40 percent of her body weight. On leaving her den, she is intent on feeding on spring buds and anything she can hunt or scavenge. A female with cubs is easily disturbed. Breeding males, beginning at age 5–6, although sexually mature at age 2, are potentially dangerous as they secure their territory.

Black bears, both male and female, with or without cubs, may use their dens even after coming out of winter dormancy—by way of example, a man was killed by a male black bear near its den in Québec in April 2003 (see p. 52). Whether the bear was defending the territory surrounding the den or whether it was hungry and in predatory mode when he attacked the man could not be determined with certainty.

UNDERSTANDING THE MOTIVATIONS AND DANGERS

A black bear's motivation is typically governed by hunger, as this species does not tend to have the level of territorial aggressiveness typical of the grizzly bear. A bear that has become habituated to human presence and food-conditioned to human food sources is the most likely cause of a bad human-bear encounter. Surprising a bear is another danger because the bear's reaction is unpredictable, and it may attack if it feels cornered or threatened. Recognizing posture and behaviour in a black bear offers clues that can guide your response in an encounter.

Defensive Behaviour

A defensive bear is a stressed bear. It is uncomfortable with your presence, which may be too close or in some other way threatening. The bear may or may not retreat and may or may not approach you. A defensive bear displays signs of feeling threatened, agitated and stressed through one or more vocal or visual cues. Huffing, woofing or popping its jaws, as well as pacing, swinging its head or slapping the ground or a tree are things to watch for. Angry growls, whining and sniffs are also likely. This situation may escalate into a bluff charge, stopping short of contact. The head will be lowered, with ears drawn back while facing you. Excessive salivation is a serious sign of aggression and typically comes just before an actual charge. All of these signs are the bear's way of warning you to retreat; it is trying to communicate to you that you are too close. ***Back away slowly, giving the bear more space.***

A **cornered bear** feels trapped or without a way to avoid you. It will use threats and behaviours such as the ones listed above to encourage you to move out of its way.

A **female black bear with cubs**, unlike a grizzly or polar bear, is rarely aggressive toward humans, and her instinct to flee from danger is stronger than the urge to attack. Biologists tagging bear cubs have observed the female making bluff charges or retreating and hiding when her cubs have been captured for tagging. There are no documented cases of humans being attacked by a female black bear with cubs, nor is there any evidence of a female attacking or stalking humans in a territorial or predatory manner, because doing so would pose too great a risk to her cubs. Nevertheless, a mother bear will be sensitive and protective; always keep a large, respectful distance from a female with cubs, and never come between them or offer any threat. Do not intentionally approach cubs or knowingly separate them from their mother. The cry of a cub in distress sounds similar to the crying of a human baby. A mother bear typically uses defensive warning signs to tell you that you are too close.

Bears that are **feeding**—at a garbage site, campsite, food cache or carcass—may also display defensive behaviour, warning you to move away. Or they may attack without warning. Similarly, bears may act attack without warning if they want food that you have (or that, by scent, they believe you have).

Offensive Behaviour

A bear displaying offensive behaviour shows little or no stress, aggression or agitation. It approaches deliberately, without the vocal or visual cues associated with defensive behaviour. An offensive bear may be asserting its dominance or simply planning to pass, or it may be curious. ***Give the bear the right of way by moving aside as far as possible and avoiding eye contact, then calmly leave the area.***

At a distance, a **curious bear** may circle downwind of you to get a better whiff of your scent, typically standing on its hind legs. When a bear stands upright on its hind legs, it is investigating your presence by sight, smell or both. The bear may or may not be threatened by you. It may show little or no fear as a result of having become habituated to human presence or human food. If it does not show you any further interest, don't give it reason to investigate more thoroughly.

Offensive behaviour and predatory behaviour have only subtle observable differences: a bear that is stalking has its head up and ears erect.

Predatory Behaviour

Predatory behaviour is the most dangerous behaviour in a black bear. Most human fatalities caused by black bears have been predatory situations. Predatory bears are most often adult males. Predatory black bears do not necessarily make any threatening postures or sounds because they do not want you to flee. Instead, they want to investigate you, and they may press closer and closer, head and ears erect, as they decide whether or not to attack.

Often, the victim is not aware of the bear until it's too late—its approach has been silent and direct. If undeterred, a predatory bear proceeds to attack with the intent to kill and consume the victim. The bear may drag the body a significant distance to another area, typically into dense brush, where it can conceal its prey from other bears or scavengers and feel secure. *Never play dead if attacked by a predatory bear— fight back with all means available.*

ENCOUNTERS

- if you see a black bear
  - stay calm and assess the situation
  - do not approach the bear
- if the bear is unaware of you
  - move away quickly, calmly and quietly, keeping your eye on the bear
- if the bear is aware of you but does not advance
  - do not run away; a flight response may excite the bear or stimulate its instinct to chase you or see you as prey, and bears can outrun you, having been clocked at up to 40 km/h (25 mph)
  - keep your eye on the bear, but do not make direct eye contact, which may be perceived as threatening

- o speak in low tones to identify yourself as human
- o back away slowly
- o keep dogs away from a bear, unless they are properly bear trained; an untrained or poorly trained dog may irritate the bear or entice it to follow the dog back to you
- if the bear is aware of you and advances
- o remain facing the bear
- o speak to it in firm, low tones
- o back or move laterally out of the bear's path
- o if you are near a building or car
  - ⊙ back toward it and get inside
- o if you do not have a car, building or safe area to retreat to
  - ⊙ find a tree or large rock that may protect you
  - ⊙ move uphill or elevate yourself onto a log or rock
  - ⊙ raise your arms to look taller
  - ⊙ do not enter a water body as solace from an attacking black bear; this animal is an excellent swimmer
  - ⊙ because black bears are excellent climbers, consider climbing a tree only as a way to make a defensive bear feel less threatened, not as a practical escape strategy when faced with a predatory animal
- o if you are with other people
  - ⊙ stay together and act as a group to deter the bear
  - ⊙ make sure the bear has a clear escape route
- o as you back away, throw things *in front* of the bear as a distraction
  - ⊙ a piece of clothing or a shoe is a good choice of something to throw
  - ⊙ do NOT throw food in front of the bear, which will then recognize you as the source; if you have food with you, throw it far away from both you and the bear (off to the side, not between you and the bear or in the direction of your escape)

- ⊙ throwing down your backpack is debateable—definitely drop it if there is food in it; otherwise, dropping it can serve as a potentially distracting object, freeing you to find shelter or leave the area, but wearing it offers some protection to your back if you are attacked
- ⊙ do not throw anything directly at a bear that is acting defensively, or you may provoke an attack
- if the bear continues to advance and is showing aggression
  - o raise your own level of aggression, increasing your level of communication from speaking in low tones to more threatening tones and perhaps using bear bangers or an air horn (see Noise Deterrents, p. 207)
  - o as the bear steps toward you, mirror this behaviour, stamping your feet on the advance
  - o if you are carrying bear spray
    - ⊙ get it in your hand, point the nozzle away from you and check the wind direction to make sure the spray will not blow back on you
    - ⊙ use bear spray only if the bear comes within close range; within 1 m (3 ft) is optimal, but 3–4 m (10–13 ft) at most (see Bear Spray, p. 201)
    - ⊙ do not use bear spray if the bear is upwind
- if the bear charges
  - o most charges are bluff charges; stand your ground while avoiding direct eye contact; do not run or turn your back
  - o do not lie down or be passive—if the bear is in predatory mode, it may investigate you as prey
  - o in a bluff charge, the bear stops short of contacting you and then begins to back away—at this point, you should also back away
  - o if the bear makes additional bluff charges
    - ⊙ continue to hold your stance during the charge

- ⊙ continue to back away after the charge until the bear is sufficiently secure that you are retreating
- if the bear attacks
- o do not play dead
- o fall to the ground immediately upon contact and protect your vital organs (a black bear kills its prey by lashing at the belly) and face; two postures are recommended
  - ⊙ lie on your stomach with your hands linked behind your neck and your face and vital organs against the ground, legs slightly splayed to give you leverage into the ground, which will make it harder for the bear to flip you over; if the bear does flip you over, roll back onto your stomach
  - ⊙ roll into a ball (fetal position, typically on your side) to protect your face and vital organs while having the mobility of your arms and legs to punch, jab and kick at the bear if the attack turns predatory, recognizable by biting and chewing
- o if the attack is defensive, the bear may back off
  - ⊙ do not move or make a sound until you are sure the bear has left—if you do, the bear may resume the attack because it still feels threatened
- o if the attack is predatory or turns predatory, the bear will begin biting and chewing your arms and legs
  - ⊙ fight back with all your force using any available weapon—knife, axe, stick, rock, binoculars, car keys or bare hands
  - ⊙ aim for the nose and eyes to deter the bear as best you can to encourage it to retreat
  - ⊙ avoid, if possible, allowing the bear to grab your arms or legs in its jaws; keep moving, avoiding and fighting back
  - ⊙ scream and yell to deter the bear and in hopes that somebody hears you
  - ⊙ be relentless—**fight for your life**

FIGHT BACK!

In his excellent book *Bear Attacks: Their Causes and Avoidances,* Stephen Herrero explains that when a black bear attacks, it is preying on you. When surprised and threatened, a black bear almost always tries to flee the scene; at most, it will attack as a strategy to help it escape. But, if a black bear keenly and deliberately approaches you, eyes focused upon you, head up and ears erect, it is stalking you as prey. If it runs at you, it is likely intending to attack; if it makes contact, it is with the intent to kill. If you play dead, the bear will proceed to eat you. Never play dead when a black bear attacks. Always fight back.

People who have wrongly been instructed or who have incorrectly thought that playing dead is the only strategy of defence in a bear attack usually soon stop playing dead and are dead. People who have survived have sometimes been partially consumed.

One example is the case of Karen Austrom, who was hiking in BC's Mount Robson Provincial Park in July 1979. She was hiking alone, which increases the odds of a black bear attack; a black bear can easily stalk an individual prey but is usually deterred by a group of people, which would be too much of a threat to the bear's own safety. Karen saw the young 57-kg (125-lb) male black bear before it attacked her. She came across the bear at close range on the trail. The bear had apparently stalled the attack, which was likely not premeditated. It even climbed a tree, whereupon Karen attempted to calmly leave the area. At some point, however, the bear changed its attitude toward Karen and pursued and attacked her. Once it did, she played dead. She offered the bear her arm in the hope of sparing the rest of her body and avoiding attack upon her head or vital organs. The bear then graciously proceeded to eat her arm! Her ability to passively endure such torture is inconceivable. Forty-five minutes later, a group of people arrived upon the gruesome scene and scared the bear off. Karen had only minor injuries to most of her body, but the sacrificial arm had been largely consumed.

Other experts agree with Herrero when he writes, "this is a clear case in which the victim should have used every possible means to fight and intimidate the bear." Karen had likely assumed that if she did not fight back, the bear would leave her for dead after no longer perceiving her as a threat, which is grizzly bear—not black bear—behaviour. A black bear will not only eat its victim, it will drag any leftovers off into the bush and bury them to eat later. Final word on black bear attacks: fight back!

UNFORESEEN DANGER

No stranger to the outdoors, Robin Kochorek grew up enjoying the wilderness of the Canadian Rockies—hiking, riding bikes, swimming, skiing and camping, making trips into the mountains with family and friends, pitching tents or sometimes sleeping under the stars. She had hiked many kilometres of trail through the Rockies with her father Bob, and they were always planning their next trip. Robin and her dad revelled in the wilderness together.

The Kochorek family owned property in Windermere, near Invermere in eastern BC's Rocky Mountains, and that is where Robin spent most summers romping about in the woods and most winters skiing at the Panorama Mountain Village resort. She was athletic—a bicycle commuter, former gymnastics coach and younger sister to two rough-and-tumble brothers—but she was not a risk taker.

One typical sunny summer day in July 2007, while out biking the trails in Windermere with her brother Michael and friend Lindsay, Robin would make a fateful decision to take an easier, safer route. It was a day when a mid-morning bike ride seemed a good proposal, and Robin had decided at the last minute to join the other two nature buffs. They had picked a popular biking route in a well-used summer recreational area in the Panorama Mountain Village. Near the conclusion of their ride, the trail branched into two runs: a challenging intermediate run and an easy novice run. Michael and Lindsay were eager for the challenge of the harder route, but Robin opted for the latter choice. The three planned to meet at the bottom of the trail in an hour and then head home for lunch. Robin never arrived.

Search parties, armed with bear spray and fearing the worst, began looking for Robin that afternoon, but it took a helicopter flying over the area the next morning to finally locate her. A small, tan-nosed black bear was found guarding Robin's body in a clearing near the path she had been riding. She knew the area well and had apparently intentionally chosen this path, which was an unofficial detour about 400 m (440 yd) from the mountain-biking trail. Somewhat of a logging and access road, it was used in winter as a connective corridor between cross-country ski paths.

Investigation reports say there was no sign of struggle; the bike was undamaged on the path near the clearing where Robin was found. Investigators believe that it had been a surprise, face-to-face encounter. Robin was travelling slowly up a section of the path that went uphill. Likely she had been looking down as she pedalled and hadn't seen the bear in time to defend herself, let alone attempt to deter the animal or consider her escape. When it attacked, the bear would have taken advantage of her slow pace, her stooped and downward-facing posture and her solitary situation. The incident would have ended very quickly, and the bear dragged its prey off into the bush.

The RCMP shot the bear at the scene. An autopsy on Robin confirmed that the bear had attacked and killed her, and a necropsy of the bear showed it contained human remains. The bear was four years old, weighing about 90 kg (200 lb) and in normal condition. It is unknown why this healthy bear had such an aggressive disposition and the confidence to attack a human, but all the details of the attack confirm that it was a classic case of predatory black bear behaviour.

"It's easy to forget how powerful, dangerous and unpredictable these bears can be," explained Paul Visentin, a Cranbrook-based conservation officer with the BC Ministry of Environment who was involved with the investigation. "Normally we look for reasons, such as a sow [female bear] with cubs, maybe a wildlife kill nearby, protecting a berry patch, a wounded bear situation. We looked at all the triggers that we would normally associate to this and we just didn't find any. We feel this bear is an aggressive bear and it was just an accident waiting to happen," he concluded.

Robin's brother Michael stated after the accident that if there had been warning signs, they wouldn't have ridden the trails. "My sister was the type of person that would never go out of bounds. If anything, she made a decision to take a pre-caution and go on a green run. Unfortunately, she came upon a bear as a result of that," he said.

A spokesperson for Panorama Mountain Village resort provided the following statement: "We are in the wilderness, as are a lot of these parks and resorts, and there are going to be bears around."

It soon came to light that the bear that had attacked Robin had been demonstrating aggressive behaviour and had been reported three times in the area by mountain bikers who had encountered it and believed that it was either following them or not fleeing in a manner typical of black bears. Warning signs had been posted earlier in the week following these reports but were later removed, and Robin had not known of the possibility of an aggressive bear in the area.

Speculation was that the bear had become habituated to the high number of people in the area. If the bear was having difficulty avoiding human encounters, it may have become overly confident around people and perhaps irritated by the frequency of encounters. In the four years of the bear's life, there is no previous evidence that it had been problematic. Something had recently changed to cause the hostility in its behaviour. Unfortunately, with high human and bear densi-ties in the same area, the frequency of encounters is also high. In such a situation, it can be difficult to gauge when to con-sider a bear a nuisance and attempt to relocate it. Sadly, the response in reaction to this particular bear was too late to save Robin's life.

This case remains somewhat controversial as to whether resort authorities acted irresponsibly, and whether they should have reported the bear to conservation officials and been more diligent in warning the public about the bear.

In her 31 years, Robin had travelled the world and been in places and situations where her family feared for safety. Several stories were told in the many eulogies and exchanges of fond memories between friends of how Robin had been mugged and robbed while travelling in Africa and South America, through places where she had been in seemingly much greater danger. She was an adventurous woman, and her family never stopped worrying until she was safely at home. It is still unfathomable that she died only 25 minutes from her home.

In the many newspaper reports about Robin's death, Canadians learned about her and her love for nature. Her brother Michael spoke to reporters about his family taking solace in the fact that Robin was happiest when outdoors, hiking or riding her bike, and that is what she had been doing in her final moments. Friends told of how Robin started an environmental club when attending the University of Alberta and inspired them all to get more active. All who knew her told stories of her adventurous spirit that inspired her world travels; she lived life to the fullest while remaining compassionate and generous. Her family has established a trust called "Robin's Nest," a legacy to help disadvantaged children, a cause Robin was dedicated to helping.

THE RIVER RUNS WILD

Coursing northward through Ontario, the Missinaibi River runs wild and free. One of Canada's celebrated unspoiled rivers, it is one of the province's longest free-flowing wilderness waterways. Its source is Missinaibi Lake, and it joins the Mattagami River to become the Moose River corridor to James Bay, pouring its fresh water into the salty subarctic brine. Experienced canoeists and kayakers revel in riding its white waters as they follow a historic fur-trading route. It is not a river for the inexperienced—it drops 330 m (1080 ft) while crossing the Canadian Shield, with a striking 60-m (200-ft) plunge at Thunderhouse Falls, where a number of unfortunate river navigators have met their demise after failing to pull ashore in time. The upper Missinaibi River and Missinaibi Lake are part of the Chapleau Crown Game Preserve, the largest game preserve in the world at 7000 km^2 (2700 mi^2). It is home to 8–10 wolf packs that are sustained by some 2500 moose, along with other prey species. This boreal preserve is also inhabited by approximately 2000 black bears.

Thousands of people per year visit the park, with many camping in the remote backcountry, so the number of human-bear encounters is quite high. Yet, most such meetings are without incident, and, before 2005, there had never been a bear-caused fatality or even serious injury. Most visitors are more concerned about surviving the rapids or—even more frightening—the half-million blackflies per square metre that can occur in some areas.

But one black bear was not enjoying the day as much as the numerous tourists were on September 6, 2005. Perhaps he was getting annoyed with how many people were crossing his path—we can only speculate. No longer a young bear, he had become familiar with human presence, possibly too familiar, and had lost his fear of people.

The clean, highly oxygenated waters of the Missinaibi system provide superb river and lake habitat for walleye, northern pike, lake trout, speckled trout, rainbow trout, splake, yellow perch, lake whitefish and smallmouth bass, and subsequently, excellent opportunities for anglers—and bears. Apparently, this bear went down to the lakeshore to do a little fishing of his own when he found two fishermen already there.

The men left the area and moved to a different fishing spot. A short while later, the bear left the water and meandered along a trail, whereupon he encountered another two men, a father and son from Philadelphia on a camping holiday. They began yelling at the bear and waving their arms. Eventually, they managed to deter the bear and scare it off by hitting an axe against a picnic table.

Possibly quite agitated by the day's events, the bear travelled another 500 m (550 yd) southeast along the lakeshore. Less than an hour later, the bear encountered two more people—perhaps just two too many—and attacked.

The unfortunate recipients of the bear's displeasure were a young married couple, Jacqueline Perry and Mark Jordan, both 30 years old. Jacqueline, a family doctor at Grandview Medical Centre in Cambridge, Ontario, was due to start working in emergency medicine when she returned from this romantic nature retreat with her husband. With backcountry camping and kayaking down the Missinaibi, it was to be two weeks of peace and tranquillity in nature before entering into this new and demanding phase of her promising medical career.

When the bear arrived, Jacqueline and Mark were setting up camp at a campsite well into the park, about 12 km (7.5 mi) from the main campground and access point to Missinaibi Lake. They had spent the day kayaking on the lake and had just started to organize their supplies and equipment for the night on a section of the south shoreline across from Whitefish Falls. They had set their dried food bags on the picnic table near the fire pit. It was about 5:30 PM when the bear stumbled upon the scene and attacked.

The aggressive and violent attack focused on Jacqueline. Desperately, Mark repeatedly stabbed the bear with his Swiss army knife in an attempt to free his wife. Over a dozen times the bear withdrew about 3 m (10 ft), only to shortly renew the attack. Finally, a 20-cm (8-in) gash to the bear's neck deterred the animal long enough for Mark to carry Jacqueline to the kayak and begin paddling frantically in the direction of the nearest campsite.

Mark was also bleeding from numerous lacerations to his legs and right hand, and, as he paddled, he began to call out for help. Hearing his cries, the father and son from Philadelphia who had just deterred the bear half an hour earlier looked up to see Mark paddling his kayak toward them. They jumped into their rowboat and met the kayak out on the water. They transferred Jacqueline, severely mauled and unconscious, into their boat and continued to row toward the main campsite, calling for help.

They flagged down yet another boat, a pontoon boat that carried two men—an off-duty police officer and a doctor from North Carolina. Mark climbed onboard the faster boat, and they raced the rest of the way to the access point at the main campground to call for emergency assistance, while the doctor stayed with Jacqueline on the slower boat and did his best to treat her grave injuries. The Ontario Provincial Police and an ambulance arrived to meet the boat carrying Jacqueline, but she had already succumbed to her injuries. By this time, more than an hour had passed since the attack.

Staff from the Ontario Ministry of Natural Resources embarked on a search for the rogue bear, which they found at 8 AM on Saturday, September 10. They shot and killed the bear and sent the body to be tested for disease and to do a necropsy for life history information. Results came back reporting that the bear was an estimated 9–11 years old and in poor condition for early fall. He weighed 94.6 kg (208.5 lb) without the head (which was taken for rabies tests, which came back negative) and had a low amount of body fat. No other apparent physical abnormalities were found. Therefore, we can only speculate that the bear was having trouble finding adequate food sources to fatten up for winter. He was either desperate or opportunistic as well as overly habituated by frequent human encounters, making him less averse to attempting to take down human prey.

Bear experts with the ministry later stated that such attacks are very rare (only four fatalities were brought about by black bears in Ontario between 1979 and 2005) and speculated that it was a predatory attack. Officials further commented that the area where Jacqueline was attacked had had a higher than usual share of bear sightings that year. However, no fatal black bear attacks or serious injuries in this northern park had ever been reported previously—or since.

Dr. Jacqueline Perry's colleagues at the hospital where she worked were devastated. The hospital held the flag at half-mast the week of her death as they mourned the loss of a person the chief of staff described as a very respected, energetic and vibrant young physician. In 2007, Governor General Michaëlle Jean honoured Mark Jordan with the Star of Courage, which is awarded for "acts of conspicuous courage in circumstances of great peril."

BOTH BEARS AND PEOPLE MISJUDGE

At only 24 years of age, Mary Beth Miller was an accomplished and recognized biathlete, ranked fifth in Canada. She was well known and celebrated throughout the country. The pride of the Northwest Territories, where she grew up and trained, Mary Beth had been honoured the previous year as the Northwest Territories Female Athlete of 1999. She was training for her next big race when she took to the trail for a run one July 2000 morning at 9 AM. Her starting point was the Myriam Bédard Biathlon Centre at the Canadian Forces Base Valcartier (in the Capitale-Nationale region of Québec), where 40 km (25 mi) of trails specially for biathlete training have been laid out through the woods of the Laurentian Mountains. Despite all the instructions and warnings given at the base that anyone using the trails should always go with a partner, Mary Beth struck out alone.

By evening, the light was beginning to fade, and the weather had turned to rain. Mary Beth's trainer and others began to wonder why she had not returned. Patrol officers set out to look for her on the trails. They found her body on the trail, with no indication that there had been a struggle. By this time, the rain was rapidly washing away any clues, but adult bear tracks were still visible among the nearby trees. The young woman had been killed by a bite to the back of her neck, breaking it between the third and fourth vertebrae.

Officers at the scene surmised that the bear had probably chased Mary Beth along the trail for a short distance as she ran without her even realizing it. When the bear attacked, it was from behind. Coroner Yvan Turmel confirmed that the bear likely lunged at the woman first to knock her down. He attributed the gashes on the back of the victim's left hip either to the bear attacking from her left side or as a result of the woman turning to her left at the last moment, possibly hearing the bear just before it launched at her. The bear had knocked its victim to the ground and immediately grabbed her neck in its jaws, delivering a single deadly bite. Then, the bear simply left. The body had not been dragged or preyed upon in any fashion.

The search for the bear began. The week before Mary Beth was attacked, there were reports of a bear chasing two cyclists, who had escaped unharmed. Following this earlier incident, bear traps had been laid, but without success. Six traps were laid the day after the attack on Mary Beth. A young male bear was the first to be captured, but its paw and teeth did not match the marks left on Mary Beth's body.

The next day, a second bear was captured. This time it was a nursing female black bear, apparently without a cub, and it was behaving very aggressively in the cage. This bear's teeth measurements corresponded, and she was put down. Tests for rabies came back negative, and, soon after, DNA results came back to prove that this four-year-old female bear was as unfortunate as she was innocent—she was not the bear that had killed Mary Beth. The bear responsible was never officially caught, but after the accident, the Canadian Forces opened the military base to trapping. No further aggressive bears have been reported in the area.

Experts analyzing the incident concur that the bear was not likely an aggressive bear, nor was it predatory. Although it appeared to have been stalking Mary Beth, it had apparently not identified her as human. It is plausible that the bear was alongside the trail when it heard a noise and saw a figure moving fast in the forest and took a short run to take down what it may have thought to be a deer or other prey animal. After knocking down the victim, its predatory instinct caused it to carry through with the bite to the neck, but then it did not have any interest in preying upon the person, so it just left the area.

A group of people running together would most likely have intimidated the bear and prevented an attack. In addition, the runners would probably have been talking to each other, thus identifying themselves to the bear as humans.

Ironically, Mary Beth was not ignorant about bear behaviour and understood the dangers that bears pose. She had graduated in 1999 with a degree in biology and physical education. During her studies (in 1996), she had been employed as a wildlife technician on an environmental impact study on the Barren Lands, just a few hundred kilometres from her hometown of Yellowknife. While doing this study, she surveyed several species, including grizzly bears. With this experience, she had a better understanding of bear behaviour than most people. However, it is difficult to be diligent with safety precautions, and finding a running partner on every occasion is not always possible. This misjudgement to run alone down a forest trail, which she probably considered safe—and even the bear's own possible error in not correctly identifying its prey—resulted in a tragic loss of human and ursine life.

OCCUPATIONAL HAZARD

Being in top triathlete shape would have its disadvantages for Julia Gerlach when surgeons could not find enough fat on her torso to graft new flesh onto her mauled scalp. But surviving a black bear attack was a greater reward than any trophy Julia had ever striven for before.

This remarkable 27-year-old had moved to Prince George, British Columbia, from Germany nine years prior and was working for a silviculture consultant doing survey work in the BC backcountry, about 150 km (95 mi) north of Fort Nelson, in prime black bear habitat. As so often happens to people working in the field, she often became so focussed on her work that she was unable to maintain a constant vigilance for bears in her surroundings.

Although a stealthy predatory black bear is often impossible to detect, Julia actually turned to see the bear approach in time to grab her bear spray and fire it at him. Undeterred, he launched upon her. Going straight for her head, he attacked with clear intent to kill. Julia also claims to have hit the bear on the face with the empty can, aiming for the sensitive nose. Yet, the attack continued.

Remarkably, Julia continued fighting back and was even able to grab her radio and call for help. Her colleagues came running to her rescue and scared the bear off by firing a rifle. A helicopter was called to take her to Fort Nelson, and Julia was soon in the air ambulance to Edmonton, Alberta. She was immediately rushed into emergency surgery at the University of Alberta Hospital.

The damage was grave. Julia's scalp was torn away, one ear was missing and her arms and legs were so peppered with puncture wounds from the bites that it took 95 stitches to close them. The damage to her head was so severe that a plastic surgeon needed 11 hours for reconstruction using skin, tissue and arteries taken from elsewhere in her body. The first thing she asked upon awakening was if anybody had called the racing association to tell them that she wouldn't make her next race!

While in the recovery room, head completely wrapped in white bandages, Julia met the hoards of journalists, reporters, RCMP, conservation officers and spokespersons with smiles and good humour. She was happy to be alive. As she told the curious crowd, she remembered the attack vividly. Remaining conscious throughout the ordeal, she was aware of the damage that the bear was inflicting—she felt it tearing at her scalp and biting her arms and legs as she fought back—but she did not feel any pain. When her efforts to stave off the assault failed, she explained, she had the realization that she was going to die, and she hoped it would happen quickly. It was then that the bear was scared off.

Conservation officers tracked and killed what turned out to be a young bear about three years old and weighing approximately 90 kg (200 lb).

The attack had taken place on May 27, 2005, but as soon as she was released from the hospital, Julia was back in training for her next race in October, a half-Ironman. She said that the challenge of getting back into training was not as great as that of returning to the woods.

Once back at home, she went with her dog out into the cutblock behind her house, where she used to enjoy running and wanted to feel confident to do so again. She says that she remembers being nervous—and perhaps even frightened—but soon got over it.

Perhaps inspired by the idea that when you fall off a horse you have to get right back on and conquer the fear, Julia wasted little time in overcoming her own traumatic experience. She says that she has no negative feelings about the incident and that, as with every obstacle in life, good things come from the bad as well. She is healed and happy and claims that the mauling did not leave her with any deep fear of bears, but she admits to being more cautious when in their territory. She is in more ways than one a true Ironman in the eyes of all who have heard her story.

* * *

Other people in similar situations have not been so lucky to survive such a predatory black bear attack. A few years prior to Julia Gerlach's attack, there had been another case near Fort Nelson, a region familiar with human-bear conflict. The Fort Nelson lowland is a bottomland along the eastern slopes of the northern Rockies, an area of black spruce bogs, muskeg and permafrost, mixed forests of aspen and conifers and meandering streams lined with cottonwoods. This diverse habitat is ideal for black bears, forest dwellers that love dark, boggy areas free of grizzlies. Whereas Julia had been working in this remote area for the forestry industry, this victim was a young man working for the oil and gas industry.

Fort Nelson relies heavily on the extraction-based industries of oil and gas (Fort Nelson is part of the Greater Sierra oil field) along with forestry. Although the town's permanent residents number only around 5000, the population can nearly double with seasonal workers coming to log or work on oil rigs, and, from spring through fall, an estimated 14,000 tourists travel through the area. An area so desired by both black bears and people is bound to have the two species cross paths frequently—and they do. For the most part, these encounters are without incident, benign events with a typically tolerant and passive bear. Most black bears throughout North America—and there are thousands—tend to either shy away from people or seemingly pose for cameras, becoming postcard favourites of tourists. Why certain individuals so violently shatter the gentle reputation of the species as a whole remains an unanswerable question.

Christopher Bayduza was working on an oilrig just north of Fort Nelson when he was killed by a black bear in September 2002. He was employed as a directional driller with Trinidad Drilling of Lloydminster, a contractor company for oilfield services provider Halliburton Co., and had been stationed at this rig with four other men for the past month. Christopher was on his last shift before returning home to his wife and son in Ardrossan, Alberta, when he walked behind his trailer and was confronted by a black bear. Christopher's coworkers heard him yell out and came running only to see the bear dragging their mate off into the bushes. They chased after it, hurling objects at it—one man fired arrows at it with his bow—until the bear dropped Christopher and fled. The men radioed for rescue and administered first aid to Christopher's serious head and neck injuries. The situation was made more desperate by bad weather and low cloud cover that prevented an air ambulance from flying in. The time involved in waiting for the ambulance to arrive and then driving to the hospital proved to be too long, and Christopher succumbed to his injuries.

The bear was found within a couple of hours of searching for it and was shot by conservation officers. Upon necropsy, the bear was positively identified as being the bear responsible for the attack; a broken arrow head was found in a wound inflicted within hours of the bear being destroyed, and there was human flesh in its stomach. The bear was estimated at 7–10 years old. It weighed 90–100 kg (200–220 lb), had good teeth and was in generally good condition (evidence of an old pelvic injury was noted) with berries in its digestive track. The attack was concluded as predatory in nature.

Christopher was only 31 years old and a new father to his eight-month-old son, for whom the Ethan Christopher Bayduza Trust Fund was later established. Born and raised in Sherwood Park, Alberta, Christopher was a recent graduate from the University of Alberta's Environmental and Conservation Sciences program with a major in Rangeland Management. His wife and family have set up a scholarship fund in his name for promising students in this same U of A program.

*　　*　　*

In Québec, a forestry worker was killed by a black bear on April 17, 2003, while he was working in a remote forested area 10 km (6 mi) south of Waswanipi, southwest of Chibougamau. Donald Chrétien was working alone marking woodcutting areas when, whether knowingly or unknowingly, he walked within 20 m (65 ft) of a black bear den. He was not approaching the entrance but was walking in a straight line directly past when the bear emerged from the bush and chased after him, reportedly for 30 m (100 ft). The bear killed the man with heavy blows to his head and claw injuries to his body and then dragged him into its den. His body was discovered by someone who saw his feet protruding from the den.

A recovery squadron of provincial police from Lebel-sur-Quévillon and game wardens from Chibougamau Provincial Park came to the scene. When they pulled Donald's body from the den, the bear emerged and was immediately shot and killed. It was a male black bear weighing about 135 kg (300 lb). The head was removed and sent for tests for rabies, which came back negative, and the carcass was burned at the scene. This death marked the third fatality by black bear in four years in Québec; prior to that, there had only ever been a single case documented, in 1983 (see following story).

DISPELLING THE STORYBOOK IMAGE

Anybody who has ever camped in Yosemite National Park in California probably finds it hard to believe that black bears cause people any harm. We are all familiar with the images from the past century of bears being handfed on roadsides, and, although this practice is forbidden today, bears are nearly as prevalent as squirrels in the campgrounds. They boldly steal hotdogs and marshmallows from people's picnic tables—sometimes even as the people are seated at them.

In addition, bears have long been given human and sentimental personas in cartoons, nursery rhymes and stuffed toys. Winnie-the-Pooh, Baloo, Goldilocks and the Three Bears, the Bernstein Bears, Yogi Bear, Smokey the Bear, cuddly teddy bears and many more form a legion of cute and friendly characters that have been befriending children for generations. These characters have done a great deal to increase our level of fondness and compassion for these animals, but perhaps at the risk of children—and some adults—having a false understanding of the animal itself, forgetting that bears are wild and potentially dangerous animals.

The black bears in Yosemite National Park are a nuisance, but there has never been a case of one attacking a person. Elsewhere in the United States, such is not the case, and there is a record of human fatalities caused by black bears. Canada has such a record as well. In most of the provinces in which black bears are found, there has been at least one case of an injury or fatality in recent history. The exception is Nova Scotia, where the black bears are as docile as those in Yosemite and have never so much as scratched a person. These behavioural differences between populations are not yet understood.

A smattering of campground tragedies have been documented in Canada in which children are the victims of predatory black bears. For example, on September 1, 1976, a 10-year-old girl near William's Lake, BC, was attacked and injured by a black bear while she was carrying a bucket of water from a creek up to her cabin. She saw the bear approaching her and dropped the bucket, grabbed an axe that was lying on the ground near her and actually hit the bear on the head with it! She then ran for the cabin, but the bear ran after her and swatted her to the ground. She managed to continue her retreat from the bear and got inside the cabin, grabbed the pot of water that was boiling on the stove and threw it into the bear's face. The bear then turned tail and fled. Other than the remarkable bravery of the little girl, what is noteworthy here is the explicit predatory behaviour of the bear.

A more recent incident in BC occurred in August 1999 in Rosebery Provincial Park. A black bear heard the sounds of a baby inside a tent and tore through to get at it. The child's mother was able to fend off the bear, but the baby was injured. It is possible that the similarity of a human baby's cry to that of a black bear cub in distress invoked the predatory instinct in a male bear—males prey upon and cannibalize the young of their own species, which is one reason that female bears need to be so protective.

In 1958, a seven-year-old girl was killed by a black bear in a campground in Jasper National Park, Alberta.

In July 1980, a 12-year-old boy was killed by a black bear while fishing on Leo Creek near Takla Lake, about 200 km (125 mi) northwest of Vanderhoof, BC.

In July 1983, a 12-year-old boy was camping with a group of other children and an adult camp leader in La Vérendrye Wildlife Reserve on Lac Canimina in Québec when he was pulled from his tent in the middle of the night. Reportedly, the campers were aware of a bear in the area and made plenty of noise until they finally fell asleep at around 3 AM. The bear apparently waited for all to be quiet and then ripped through one of the tents and grabbed the young boy, dragging him off and killing him before any of the other campers had time to react.

On July 15, 1997, an 11-year-old boy was injured in a similar incident in Algonquin Provincial Park in Ontario.

The preceding cases are all examples of predatory black bear behaviour in which the bear has sized up its prey and found it to be small and unthreatening enough to stalk. Always keep children close to adults when playing, hiking or biking in bear country. When tenting, have the children sleep alongside an adult in a tent and not alongside the edge of tent if possible. Children fall victim to predatory black bears more easily than adults simply because they are smaller and weaker than adults. Bears may or may not perceive this advantage because attacks on children do not necessarily occur in greater frequency than attacks on adults, but children are less likely to survive.

The Weak Attacking the Weak

Attacks on the elderly add some credence to the likelihood that the bears do perceive weakness in human prey, just as they would in animal prey—black bears prey upon young, sickly and weak or aged ungulates as well. One example comes from Québec, where an elderly man was killed by a black bear in 2002.

In September 2002, a 77-year-old man and his two sons went out to their hunting cabin on the Patapédia River on the Gaspé Peninsula. The Malenfant men had a tradition of coming out to their cabin every fall for hunting moose using bow and arrow. The elder Malenfant had retired from the hunt but still enjoyed coming out to appreciate the woods and spend time with his two sons. While the younger men were out patrolling the woods and stalking game, Mr. Malenfant would sometimes drive his pickup truck out to favourite spots to relax, watch a sunset or contemplate a scenic vista. From a swampy area of the woods, one of the sons saw his father drive past on his way back to the cabin from one of these sojourns, and he decided to also head back and join him at the cabin. He walked back to his ATV and drove back on the same road on which his father had just passed. He was likely back within half an hour of his father's arrival.

When the younger man arrived, his father's truck was parked in front of the cabin. However, within that brief passage of time, a black bear near the cabin had seen an opportunistic prey possibility. The elderly Malenfant walked stiffly and with a significant stoop in his posture, his back arched and his face looking to the ground. Because he was likely looking downward, he probably did not see the bear approach. Even if he had noticed the bear, he would not have had the strength to fend off the attack, which took place in front of the cabin, as shown by the blood and the man's hat on the ground.

Tracks left on the ground and the unfortunate man's shoes showed the direction in which he had been dragged—a short distance of about 15 m (50 ft). The son spotted the bear and grabbed a gun. Through the attached scope he saw the body of his father lying at the bear's feet. He shot the bear dead, but it was too late to save his father, who had been killed by the initial bites to his head and neck.

The bear was sent to a lab for necropsy, which came back with a plausible explanation for the attack. The animal's right femur had been fragmented into several pieces by a gunshot no more than a month prior. It would have been at the height of blueberry season, when people out picking berries sometimes carry guns for self-defence against bears. However, no reports had been made to the conservation offices or the RCMP in the area of a bear being shot or causing reason to be shot. Although the bear's wound was healing, the injury had likely handicapped the bear's efforts at hunting or even walking any distance in search of food and undoubtedly caused the bear significant pain and discomfort. At an estimated 5–6 years old, the male bear weighed 80 kg (175 lb), with only 1 cm (0.5 in) of fat under his skin—not an ideal condition prior to winter dormancy. The necropsy did reveal that the bear's intestines contained about 7 kg (15 lb) of blueberries, which would have been one of the few things the bear would have been able to rely upon for food. Taking all the circumstances into account, the attack on the elderly man was determined to have been predatory in nature.

After the incident, the Malenfant son stated that, prior to being shot, the bear showed no indication of being nervous as a result of his presence. We can speculate that the bear may have been somewhat habituated and that he was drawn to the general area by its level of human activity and food sources, although the Malenfant men kept the area around their cabin free of garbage, bait or animal carcasses and kept their food in a cooler in the pantry.

Another report from that summer, one month prior to the Malenfant attack, came from a fishing camp 3 km (2 mi) away from the Malenfant cabin. Salmon run in the Patapédia River, and a fisherman was washing his catch along the shore when he spotted a bear 3 m (10 ft) away. He describes how he yelled and ran away with his salmon under his arm! (Please note this is NOT the way to react to a bear encounter.)

The intrigued bruin followed the man, but the fishing camp supervisor came to the angler's aid and shooed the bear away with a broom. When the other members of the camp grabbed noisemakers and ran to their cars and bombarded the bear with car horns, car alarms and every other loud noise they could make, the bear fled the area.

There were enough people in the camp that a cook had been hired to prepare meals. The morning's breakfast had been a hefty serving of bacon and eggs, the aromas of which wafted far from the camp. It is plausible that a bear could become easily habituated with many people around and the strong scents of human food to lure it.

The time of the fishing camp incident was very near to the possible time of the gunshot injury to the bear that killed Mr. Malenfant. There was speculation was that there might be a connection between the two incidents, but the case is weak. Any number of bears could be drawn to the area by abundant blueberries in the bushes, fish in the river and human camps cooking pungent foods such as bacon and fish.

Bear-caused human fatalities are very rare in Québec, and likely the most significant factor in causing the behaviour in the bear that killed Mr. Malenfant was the injured femur. That the Malenfant bear was shot implies either poaching or a defence shooting. Either way, an irresponsible firearm user made life very difficult for this bear and is hence responsible for the starvation that led to it killing Mr. Malenfant. Handicapped, the animal could not properly feed itself, resulting in a desperate action with tragic consequences. Because the person who shot this bear in the leg did not report the incident, it is likely that there was no just cause for shooting, and perhaps the bear was far enough away that the shooter didn't even realize a hit was made.

Carrying a gun comes with the responsibility of knowing when it is appropriate to shoot and how to shoot to kill, not just injure. Understandably, if shooting saves a human life, it is unfortunate but necessary, but shooting a bear to injure and not kill is not an act of kindness. Moreover, when injured, a bear may be more dangerous if it becomes panicked or enraged, perhaps attacking the gunman in self-defence. When deterring a bear with a gunshot, the objective is to scare it into fleeing by noise or by impact nearby, not by injuring the animal. By crippling the bear that would go on to kill Mr. Malenfant, a careless or mean-spirited shooter caused a great deal of suffering to both the bear and the Malenfant family.

UNLEASHED REACTIONS

Although it may seem innocent and benign to let dogs run off-leash in the countryside, it can invite a dangerous situation. For example, because of such an unleashed dog incident in June 1998, New Brunswick came close to losing its unblemished record of zero bear-related human deaths.

Even though New Brunswick is a province with a healthy population of about 16,000 black bears, no human fatalities by black bear have ever been documented. In contrast, 15–40 bears per year are relocated as DLPs, and about the same number are destroyed (in 2006, 16 bears were killed as nuisance animals). The killing of bears in defence of property is far more prevalent than killing in defence of human life. In addition, several hundred bears die annually as a result of bear hunting (the 2006 hunt took 1924 black bears—over 1400 during the spring season with the remainder in fall, of which less than 100 were taken during the bow-only season). Collisions with motor vehicles kill additional black bears (83 in 2006). With the combination of these three factors, bears are definitely on the losing team when tallying up the victims on either side of the human-bear cohabitation issue.

Human injury, although rare, has occurred in New Brunswick. One relatively recent and severe case happened on June 2, 1998, when two dogs provoked a bear. The woman who was injured was walking on a road through a wooded area and had allowed her dogs to run off-leash, which is illegal on public property in New Brunswick, but nonetheless it happens all the time. The regulation is near impossible to enforce, and most people fail to see the harm in allowing domestic animals to run about chasing wildlife such as birds (which may be nesting) and mammals such as rabbits and rodents, or munching down a few frogs or salamanders for fun. We won't get further into that debate in this story, but the point is that an unleashed dog can flush out much more than just a harmless pheasant or rabbit.

In this incident, Spot and Rover dashed off into the woods and flushed out a very irritated black bear. Obviously, they were not bear-trained dogs. First they harassed the bear, enraging it and provoking it into chasing them. Then the hapless canines ran back to their unsuspecting master, leading the angry bear directly to her. The dogs continued to run past their owner, who then took the full brunt of the bear's assault while the dogs proceeded to the safety of home. The bear stopped in front of the woman, reared onto its hind legs and lashed out at her, knocking her to the ground and causing severe injury to her head, face and shoulders.

The bear then left. It had no intention of preying on the woman. The bear had relayed its message not to mess with it and returned back to its own business. The woman survived and was able to make her way back to her house to find her two dogs waiting patiently on her doorstep for her return.

The Hampton office of the Department of Natural Resources and Energy was called at approximately 7 PM on the evening of the attack, and personnel came immediately to set up traps in the area, which was patrolled until after dark and then all day every subsequent day until the morning of June 8, when an adult black bear was captured and destroyed.

The consequences speak for themselves. The official report made by the department tallied 133 person-hours involved in capturing and destroying the bear. One woman was near fatally injured, had to be hospitalized and will remain scarred for life. One adult bear that had never before had a negative incident with humans was killed. Negative publicity and misconceptions about bear safety arose after the incident. Two dogs remained ignorant of the damage they had caused, and two leashes had alibis proving their noninvolvement in the events.

ALGONQUIN'S SECRETS

Still, blue waters of the lake reflect the bright burnt hues of fall's maples, tamaracks and red oaks in contrast to the otherwise coniferous evergreen shores. Clouds float and birds fly past in the reflection, and you see your face looking back at you from this seemingly parallel universe. The looking glass is shattered by the blade of your canoe paddle, bringing your gaze back from the other side just in time to see a beaver. It dives below the surface, perhaps into that mysterious world that held your imagination a moment ago and smacking its tail as if slamming shut the door to prevent you from following. A bull moose peers up at the commotion, oblivious to your daydreams as it grazes on aquatic vegetation, much of which is hanging from its massive antlers, polished and dripping with water. This is the magic of Ontario's Algonquin Provincial Park, where thousands of people come to daydream away an idle day in a canoe.

Within the enchantment of Algonquin lakes are mysterious, grim events in the park's history. It was while canoeing on the aptly named Canoe Lake that the famous Canadian artist Tom Thomson met his mysterious death in 1917. It is commonly believed that he drowned, but the circumstances are vague, and the true cause remains a mystery shrouded with theories of foul play. With all the irony of any great mystery, 90 years later, in fall 2007, Algonquin claimed another great Canadian artist, Ken Danby. He collapsed and died while on a canoe trip with his family on Algonquin's North Tea Lake. However, other tales of tragedy in this park remind us of different, very real, albeit very rare, dangers in the woods—bears.

On October 11, 1991, Lake Opeongo, the park's largest lake, would take its turn as the site of tragic death. Fall is truly the best time of year at Algonquin, with the colours of the leaves, the lack of insects and the sensuous, lazy decadence of the twilight season before the long winter slumber. Opeongo's waters hold numerous islands, creating a labyrinth of watery routes to navigate by canoe.

That day, 32-year-old Raymond Jakubauskas and 48-year-old Carola Frehe climbed into their canoe to enjoy a scenic paddle out to Bates Island. Neither canoeist lived to tell the tale of their fate, and there are no witnesses as to what exactly happened to Raymond and Carola. What is understood, though, is that they were preyed upon by a large male black bear.

Because the pair had planned to be in the park and out of contact for several days beyond October 11, a search party was not organized until five days after the attack. Not knowing exactly where the canoeists might be, the would-be rescuers explored a number of islands that the two could have visited before they found the right one.

Evidence of a struggle marked the otherwise neat campsite set on the scenic shore of the lake. The couple's tent was pitched, and preparation of their evening meal had been underway when the attack occurred. The victims' partially consumed bodies were found in the bushes 300 m (330 yd) away, with scattered debris brushed overtop. The bear that had killed them was found soon after and shot. The necropsy revealed that it was a healthy adult male and that the incident was an obvious case of predation. The welts and bruises on the bear indicated that one of the victims had attempted to fight the bear off with a canoe paddle. Whoever was attacked first was likely stalked and was probably killed quickly, before the other person could mount a counterattack. Although the second person clearly had time to attack the bear, the bear proved to be overpowering.

The shocking and tragic news of this attack brought up memories of the last bear attack in the park, which had occurred in 1978. That attack had also been predatory. Such cases are extremely rare. Thousands of people come to Algonquin for their recreation every year without incident. It is easy to become complacent. The 1978 attack took the lives of three teenage boys. Some people consider the attack to have been more than predatory—the unusually aggressive bear involved apparently engaged in a killing frenzy.

On May 13, 1978, four teenage boys set out to spend a wholesome day fishing in the park. Richard Rhindress was 18 at the time, and he had brought along his 16-year-old brother Billy, Billy's friend George Halfkenny, 15, and George's younger brother Mark, 12. They were local boys and had come to a part of the park that was familiar to them, parking their car on a dirt logging road conveniently near a number of streams. They fished along several streams that day, and it was at 5:30 in the afternoon when they tried their luck on Stone Creek. By then, Richard had decided to call it quits and returned to the car for a nap, a decision that likely saved his life.

An hour later, he awoke and called to the other boys to come back and head home. He received no reply. He honked the car horn. Again, no reply. He walked out to the stream and didn't see the other boys, so, increasingly distressed, he drove along the road calling for them. After finding no sign of them, he drove to Canadian Forces Base Petawawa, where the boys' fathers were stationed.

The men went searching, but by then darkness was settling in, and they could not find the boys either. They knew something was terribly wrong, though; the boys would not have simply wandered away for no good reason. Something had surely happened to them. A large search party was organized, with over 200 men scouring the area on foot and by helicopter. The area was heavily forested with brush and trees that limited visibility; it took two entire days before the bodies of the three youths were found.

George was discovered first. Apparently, a bear had ambushed him as he walked along a trail. Although there were some signs of a struggle, apparently it had not been raucous enough to have alerted the other boys. After killing George, the bear had dragged his body into the bushes farther upstream. Investigators surmised that the other two boys were unaware of George's fate and had been ambushed by the same bear in turn. Soon after George was found, the bear was discovered feeding on the bodies of the other two boys. The bear ran off upon seeing the men approach but soon returned to reclaim its prey. At that point, the bear was shot.

Like the later attack, authorities were left to investigate three deaths that occurred without a surviving human witness. What happened that day is another of Algonquin's secrets. Details as to how the boys' bodies were found have over time become vague and are largely hearsay. Many unanswered questions leave this tragedy as another unsolved mystery. If the act was predatory, why did the bear not stop with the first victim? It has been said that George was carrying fish in his pockets, yet, according to the few details still available about this case, the bear left the fish untouched. The bear had only dragged George away and left him hidden in the bushes without returning to him even during the two days that elapsed between the attack and the arrival of the search party. The bear was reported to be a 125-kg (275-lb) male in healthy post-winter condition; it was supposedly well fed with apparently ample natural food sources of berries and fish in the area.

These three boys and the pair of canoeists mentioned earlier are victims like no others in the park's recorded history. Both these tragedies left many people grasping for explanations as to why they had happened. The victims had seemingly done nothing to provoke the attacks. Thousands of people and hundreds of bears have shared the park without incident for over a century. Were these predatory males simply two rogue bears that are completely uncharacteristic members of an otherwise timid species? All we are left with in conclusion is that all species that exhibit predatory behaviour at times, humans included, are unpredictable.

Grizzly Bear

Ursus arctos
brown bear
ours grizzli or *ours brun* in French, *aklark* in Inuktitut;
  shih in Gwich'in

Intolerant of human presence, the grizzly bear is a rarely seen icon of the West. Although grizzlies avoid human encounters with greater deliberateness than the other two species of bear in Canada, they often react aggressively if an unforeseen encounter with a human does occur at too close a range. The size of a grizzly's "personal space" can be significant indeed; grizzlies have been known to charge from hundreds of metres. If human presence is significant, grizzly bears avoid areas of otherwise ideal habitat, which threatens the health of this vulnerable species (see definition in Terminology, p. 216).

Grizzlies that cannot avoid humans have no alternative but to become habituated, which greatly increases the chance of encounters that may result in serious injury or death to people and death to bears. With high densities of both grizzlies and humans in BC and Alberta's Rockies, these two provinces have been the location of almost all fatal encounters that humans have had with these mighty bruins in Canada. As of this writing, only one other fatality by a grizzly bear occurred outside of these two provinces, and that was in the Yukon in 1996.

Because this book focuses on worst-case scenarios, it risks giving the impression that human proximity to a grizzly always results in human injury or death. Please don't allow this one-sided—and therefore inaccurate—representation of grizzlies to ruin your ability to relax and enjoy being in wilderness areas in which grizzlies are present. Although it is important to know how to reduce the chances of an attack, grizzly attacks are very rare. Since 1970, only a dozen grizzly-related fatalities have been documented in Canada.

The rarity of grizzly attack is well illustrated by renowned grizzly bear expert Stephen Herrero, who wrote in his book *Bear Attacks*, "We put in more than ten thousand hours working with the densest population of grizzly bears in Banff National Park. Eighty percent of the time we were on foot, visiting areas where grizzly bears had recently been active. We worked unarmed except when visiting carcasses where grizzlies might be nearby or when checking traps set for grizzlies. If grizzlies wanted to attack us, they had ample opportunity."

The Craighead brothers were pioneers of grizzly bear study in the mid-1900s. Working in Yellowstone Park (mostly in Wyoming), they tagged and handled hundreds of grizzlies and traversed over 260,000 km (162,000 mi) on foot through grizzly territory without any grizzly-inflicted injuries. As an example of a close call that also did not result in injury, early in his career, Dr. Ian Stirling, today one of Canada's most highly esteemed bear biologists, was working for the warden service in BC, clearing deadfall in an area of Kootenay National Park in June 1960, when he heard the "sporadic puffing" of a grizzly and then an angry roar just before it charged him. Ian dove into a thicket and played dead. The bear prodded at his leg, waited a few minutes, then walked away when it was satisfied that the man posed no threat. Karsten Heuer, while on his epic Yellowstone-to-Yukon hike along the Rockies, which began in 1998 and lasted 18 months, walked 3540 km (2200 mi) as part of his campaign for the identification and management of connective migratory corridors for grizzlies and other far-ranging species. Although he had encounters with grizzlies during the 188 days in which he traversed grizzly territory, he was never the victim of an attack.

Despite these stories of grizzly encounters without serious incident, always remember that we share a large part of the country with bears that are easily capable of killing a person—and, ever so rarely, one does. There is no guarantee that doing all the right things will save a person from injurious or fatal attack, but perhaps knowing a few basic details about these awesome bears can improve your odds against a serious encounter, thus protecting both yourself and the bears.

BASIC IDENTIFICATION

Height to shoulder: 90–120 cm (3–4 ft)

Total length: 1.8–2.6 m (6–8½ ft)

Tail length: 7.5–18 cm (3–7 in), but hidden beneath the long, shaggy fur

Weight: *male:* 110–525 kg (240–1160 lb), avg. 225 kg (500 lb); *female:* smaller, avg. 160 kg (350 lb)

Fore paw: 13–18 cm (5–7 in) long; 10–23 cm (4–9 in) wide

Fore paw claws: 5–10 cm (2–4 in) long; light coloured

Hind paw: 23–40 cm (9–16 in) long; 13–27 cm (5–10½ in) wide

Stride: 61–104 cm (24–41 in)

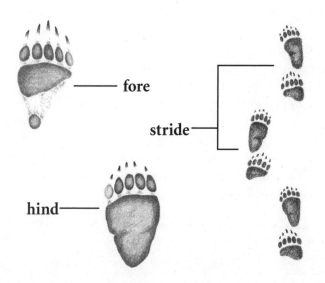

fore

stride

hind

Canada's grizzly bear gets its name from the grizzled look that the white-tipped guard hairs give to its fur, which is most often brown but can vary to almost black—which can lead to misidentification as a black bear—or to light shades such as blond, honey or even white (many white individuals gave the name White Grizzly Wilderness to an area in the Selkirk Mountains of BC). Typically, the colouration is lighter on the back and darker on the legs and belly.

The main diagnostic features of this bear are the concave facial profile, small, round ears, large, muscular shoulder hump and conspicuously long, light-coloured front claws (the latter two features endow the grizzly with strength and tools for digging). The highly adaptable grizzly has developed diverse populations throughout its Canadian range that illustrate distinct life histories in adaptation to varying ecosystems. For example, coastal grizzlies, which have higher protein diets because of the salmon they eat and a longer foraging season, are notably larger than their inland cousins. In contrast, barren-ground grizzlies on the tundra of the Northwest Territories, which have the shortest foraging season, low productivity of food sources on the barrens and the longest winter dormancy period of grizzlies in Canada, are relatively smaller in size than both inland and coastal populations.

Some experts recognize these various population ecotypes as subspecies, but the only population in North America that is genetically isolated is Alaska's large Kodiak bear (*U. a. middendorffi*). The Kodiak brown bear population is thought to have been isolated since the end of the most recent glaciation, about 12,000 years ago. The subspecies designation of the rest of the continent's grizzlies, based upon DNA, is *U. a. horribilis*; however, some people prefer to divide them into various subspecies based upon life history patterns.

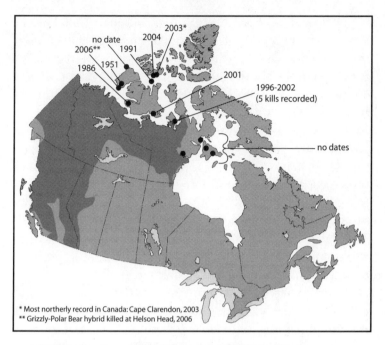

* Most northerly record in Canada: Cape Clarendon, 2003
** Grizzly-Polar Bear hybrid killed at Helson Head, 2006

WHERE CAN YOU EXPECT TO ENCOUNTER A GRIZZLY BEAR?

The brown bear, more commonly known as the grizzly in Canada (and to a lesser degree in the United States), is circumpolar in world distribution. It currently ranges from the arctic coast down into the central parts of Europe, Asia and North America. Historically, the brown bear was found throughout most of the northern hemisphere as far as northern Africa. Today, populations in China and western Europe are significantly endangered, and the most far-flung remnant populations still survive in parts of the Middle East and even Japan. In North America, although the grizzly now is not found much south of the Canada–U.S. border, its range once extended as far south as northern Mexico. The largest brown bear populations are in Russia (about 120,000 individuals), the U.S. (about 32,500, with 95 percent being the Kodiaks of Alaska) and Canada (about 29,000).

Of Canada's roughly 29,000 grizzlies, up to 17,000 live in BC, with the next significant population in the Yukon (estimated at 6000–7000). The remainder of Canadian grizzlies are found in the Northwest Territories, Nunavut and Alberta on the eastern slopes of the Rockies, with very small numbers inhabiting Alberta's Swan Hills.

In BC, grizzlies inhabit most of the province, but they are absent from Vancouver Island and Haida Gwaii (Queen Charlotte Islands), and few or none are believed to range into the Lower Mainland or the dry southern areas. Alberta is home to grizzlies only in the west, mainly in the Rocky Mountain region and the Swan Hills; a DNA census of Alberta's grizzlies to estimate grizzly population and density was conducted from 2004 to 2006 and proved the population to be less than half of the sustainable target of 1000, and, as of 2006, a three-year moratorium on hunting grizzlies was put into effect in the province. Unfortunately, for at least a decade prior to the census, Alberta's grizzlies were managed (or mismanaged) according to the inaccurate population estimate of 1000 individuals, which pushed the species to precariously low numbers. Alberta now hosts less grizzlies than Yellowstone National Park in the United States, where an estimated 600 grizzlies now live. The bear was recovered from the brink of extinction in that portion of its range.

Grizzlies range throughout the Yukon from its borders with BC and Alaska to Herschel Island and as far as Melville Island and the surrounding sea ice off the arctic coast. They inhabit the Mackenzie Mountains and Mackenzie Delta and range across the barrens of the Yukon, Northwest Territories and Nunavut.

Since the first Europeans arrived on the North American scene, the range of the grizzly (with the exception of the Kodiak) has undergone a drastic decline. The population of grizzlies that roamed the prairies, ranging as far east as Manitoba's Red River Valley, was referred to as the plains grizzly. Now believed extirpated from its range, it was last seen for

certain in the Peace River District in the 1930s, with unsubstantiated sightings in the Pasquia Hills of Saskatchewan in the 1960s.

With a life history similar to that of the plains grizzly in finding its ecological niche beyond the forests and mountains, the barren-ground grizzly population is well adapted to survival on the tundra. The challenging environment has resulted in a less robust grizzly population, but it has to some degree been less disturbed by human population encroachment, although wildlife habitats on the tundra are being negatively affected in many ways by the various mining industries.

The barren-ground grizzly occurs over the northern and eastern Mackenzie District and the central portion of the Keewatin District. The Northwest Territories recognizes three additional geographical populations of grizzlies: arctic, Richardson Mountains and northern interior. The first is in the arctic region, in coastal areas between Inuvik and Coppermine, becoming abundant on Richards Island west of

the Tuktoyaktuk Peninsula. The second lives in the Richardson Mountains and extends throughout the northern Yukon to the Alaska border. The northern interior population extends into the southern Mackenzie District, with the bulk of its range in northern BC and across most of the Yukon. Ranges into Nunavut diminish toward the east but are believed to be expanding. The bears currently occupy most of the mainland, throughout the Kitikmeot and Baffin regions and all but the northeast of the Kivalliq (the bears do not inhabit the Boothia and Melville Peninsulas, the southwest tip of Victoria Island or the coastal fringe south of Chesterfield Inlet where polar bears frequent). Several sightings outside of this range do not include female denning bears; therefore, they are not considered inhabited range. Ranges of individual grizzly bears in Nunavut are the largest reported in North America.

Both habitat productivity, which is lower in northern and high-altitude situations, and the density of potential mates affect the density of grizzlies. In the Northwest Territories, the minimum density of grizzly bears is estimated at 0.35 bears per 100 km^2 (0.91 bears per 100 mi^2); at least 800 bears are believed to inhabit the territory. For comparison, in Alaska's dense Kodiak population, there are more than 25 bears per 100 km^2 (65 bears per 100 mi^2); the arctic tundra has fewer than 0.5 bears per 100 km^2 (1.3 bears per 100 mi^2); the Khutzeymateen watershed on the BC coast has 7–10 bears per 100 km^2 (18–26 bears per 100 mi^2); and the BC interior supports 3–6 bears per 100 km^2 (7–8 bears per 100 mi^2).

The home ranges of male grizzlies in the northern interior are quite large, averaging 2075–5375 km^2 (800–2075 mi^2), and female ranges are typically 780–1390 km^2 (300–540 mi^2). A male barren-ground grizzly may roam even more widely, with a home range of up to 6685 km^2 (2580 mi^2). The average home range of the eastern slope and central Rockies grizzlies is 1000 km^2 (385 mi^2) for males and 500 km^2 (190 mi^2) for females. In BC, males have ranges of 60–700 km^2 (23–270 mi^2), and females have ranges of 25–200 km^2 (10–77 mi^2).

As with black bears, female grizzlies tolerate range overlap with other females, but males keep greater distances from each other unless challenging for dominance. To protect their young from predation, females with cubs avoid males.

The habitat varies somewhat for the geographically separate grizzly populations. Grizzlies prefer open areas in the mountains and foothills, BC interior valleys and northern tundra, but they may also be found in boreal forest and semi-forested areas and alpine and subalpine terrain. Food sources define habitat preferences. For instance, bears will be drawn to higher elevations in search of young, tender vegetation in flower or fruit after the vegetation on lower slopes is old, fibrous and spent. In estuaries, clearcuts, disturbed sites or recently burned sites, new growth of colonizing plant species that was not there before or significant new berry patches may draw grizzlies into new areas. Coastal rivers seasonally attract the bears to the salmon spawning grounds. Although they feed in open areas, grizzlies require tree or shrub cover to avoid human detection and close encounters and to find shelter from the sun and cold.

The Eastern Slopes Grizzly Bear Project has identified that the main grizzly bear habitat in the Central Rockies ecosystem is "patchy and occurs primarily in valley bottoms and mountain slopes. This patchiness has produced a naturally fragmented landscape where much of the area inhabited by grizzly bears consists of rock and ice." This challenging landscape requires grizzlies to roam between food sources as they become available throughout the changing seasons and to perpetually seek out random food opportunities as prompted by its omnivorous diet. As human activity and development expands farther into productive areas such as valleys and lower mountain slopes, grizzlies must roam even farther afield in search of alternative food sources or risk finding humans standing in the way of their next meal. As a result, the Eastern Slopes region is one of the most threatened grizzly habitats in Canada and is where the grizzly population has seen the most drastic decline in recent decades.

Grizzly bears are seen throughout the year except in winter, when they enter winter dormancy (see When Are Grizzly Bears in Their Dens?, p. 81). They are most active in the morning and early evening, sometimes through the night. The males are more active, far roaming and aggressive during mating season, between early May and mid-July.

WHAT DO GRIZZLY BEARS EAT?

Knowing what grizzly bears eat, where these foods are found and at what time of year is valuable knowledge in bear country. A lack of understanding or recognition of these patterns can result in uneducated hikers stumbling into dangerous scenarios.

The grizzly bear is omnivorous, but vegetation is usually a large component of its diet. Its wide, flat molars are well suited to grinding down grasses and other fibrous matter, and its incisors are adept at snipping vegetation. In contrast, the

closely related but mainly carnivorous polar bear has teeth that are distinctly adapted to biting prey and tearing flesh, without much chewing.

Berries are a vital component in the grizzly bear diet (see Plant Index, p. 220). Bearberry is an important and widespread food in spring and fall; overwintered bearberries have a higher sugar content in spring, whereas the abundant crops of fresh berries in fall are the main food source for bears fattening up for winter—individual bears have been shown to eat over 200,000 berries per day! Buffaloberry is particularly important for its widespread and multiseasonal availability; it is found on the eastern slopes of the Rockies in open lodgepole pine forests in valley bottoms, and it is very important in the Yukon, where it ripens in mid-July. Close to or west of the Continental Divide, grizzlies more often feast on currant, gooseberry, cranberry, huckleberry, bilberry, blueberry, salmonberry and blackberry. Crowberry, lowbush cranberry and mountain ash survive fall's first frosts, sustaining bears later into the season after more delicate berries have perished.

Besides berries, roots (especially hedysarum), bulbs, horsetails and grasses are important forage foods for grizzlies throughout the growing season. Plant food sources in mountain habitats are found in greater abundance on steep, south-facing slopes at lower elevations, and in spring, such places are key areas where you can expect to encounter grizzlies after they come out of hibernation. In coastal habitats, bears seek out new spring vegetation—grasses, horsetails, aquatic vegetation such as skunk cabbage and cow parsnip—in moist, low elevation areas, wetlands, seepage sites and estuaries. In late spring, grizzlies throughout their Canadian range may congregate in river valley bottoms. In mature spruce stands along streams and rivers, grizzlies search for horsetails and hedysarum roots. By late summer, roots and grasses are too fibrous to eat, so the bears move up onto avalanche slopes or groundwater seepage areas and smaller streams at higher elevations to forage on more horsetails as well as cow parsnip, glacier lily, springbeauty, valerian and grasses.

Although grizzlies eat a diet that consists largely of grasses, roots, tubers and berries, they also consume a wide range of animal species, from fish to moose to ants. Coastal grizzlies fish the salmon spawning runs, and inland bears feed on moderate fish runs in interior river basins, such as the Big Salmon and the Tatshenshini–Klu, kshu salmon runs in the Yukon; late-season chum salmon runs attract bears near the Fishing Branch River in the northern Yukon. Although grizzlies in other areas are likely to catch fish of one kind or another from time to time, most of their protein comes from other sources.

When ungulates are available, grizzlies hunt moose, elk, mountain goat, mountain sheep, caribou and muskox. It is mainly spring calves and lambs that are preyed upon. Only rarely do adult ungulates fall prey to grizzlies, which are not known to chase prey; however, caribou (*Rangifer tarandus*) is an important component of the barren-ground grizzly's diet. Throughout grizzly range, adult ungulates that are caught and eaten are usually injured, ill or elderly, although some simply have the misfortune to be in the wrong place at the wrong time, with no opportunity for escape.

Grizzlies will not turn their noses up at ungulate carcasses. Rather, they quite relish carrion and look for these carcasses along railway tracks and the sides of roads and freeways. In spring, grizzlies coming out of hibernation often investigate the bases of nearby avalanche slopes to see if any ungulates have been killed over winter and preserved by the cold snow for later eating.

With its muscular shoulders (which show as a hump) and long claws, the grizzly is a proficient digger. It employs its digging skill not only to excavate dens but also to dig out subterranean rodents, particularly ground squirrels and marmots, which tend to be common in mountainous and interior areas. These small mammals enter the grizzly's diet more significantly in fall, when the rodents are quite fat prior to going into hibernation; their portly state possibly makes them easier to catch. This bear is also quick to sniff out and loot fall caches of high-calorie treats such as whitebark pine seeds that ground squirrels have put away for winter use.

The grizzly can effortlessly flip over large rocks or fallen trees or dig out rotten logs in search of termites, ants and wasp larvae. In the form of a swat, this same strength can knock over and significantly injure a human.

In the extreme north of the grizzly's range along the arctic coast, this bear preys on seals. There is also evidence of female polar bears and cubs being killed and partially consumed by grizzlies where their ranges overlap. Conversely, grizzlies denning in this region of overlap may experience depredation by polar bears.

Grizzlies that inhabit the barren grounds of the Northwest Territories and Nunavut rely heavily on carrion from marine mammals, caribou and muskox and on leftovers from kills by humans and polar bears. They hunt caribou in spring, preying mainly on the calves. They prey upon Arctic ground squirrels, lemmings and red-backed voles; some birds (and bird eggs),

ringed seals, beached whales and various spawning fish also enter the diet. The vegetative component of their diet consists of berries, horsetails, sedges and Arctic cotton grass.

As with black bears, grizzlies can become attracted to human sources of garbage and food. To help prevent this food habituation, campgrounds in bear territory usually provide bear-proof garbage bins and educate their patrons about how to store food and dispose of waste to avoid attracting grizzlies and black bears. Many towns in grizzly country have had garbage dumps with food-conditioned grizzly bears, but most have made efforts in recent years to either close the dumps or implement deterrents such as electric fences. In more remote areas, such as in the Northwest Territories, there are fewer incidents of garbage- and food-conditioned bears, but the dump in Tungsten has had grizzlies. Away from civilization, fishing camps and remote industrial sites are more likely to be the places where grizzlies and humans have unfortunate encounters.

Watch for bear signs such as tracks, droppings (typically large, with vegetation, berries or hair—other large carnivores in grizzly territory do not have a vegetative component; large scats with berries are almost always from a bear), claw marks or stripped bark on trees, torn-up stumps, rotten logs and upturned earth. Loose piles of dirt, branches and vegetation might be covering a carcass that the bear has cached and is observing and guarding from nearby.

Learning to recognize important bear habitat based on food sources not only enhances human safety, but because human disturbance can cause grizzlies to avoid otherwise well-suited habitat and important areas of food supply, having and applying such knowledge also helps with the conservation of this sensitive species of bear.

WHEN ARE GRIZZLY BEARS IN THEIR DENS?

Grizzlies sometimes construct summer "day beds" in dense cover to rest or avoid the heat on hot days, but actual denning is something that these bears do in winter, spending the cold, fruitless season in dens that they excavate deep into the ground or that they find within rock caves or hollow trees.

To excavate a den in the ground, a grizzly needs dry, stable soil, usually on a steep slope. In the course of its excavations, a bear might move as much as 1 tonne (or ton) of earth out of the hillside. A "porch" made from the removed earth is backed by an opening about 1 m (3 ft) high and 1.5 m (5 ft) wide; this entrance is typically obscured by a stand of willow or alder with hanging branches that also shields it from snowfall. A tunnel typically 1–2 m (3–7 ft) long—but sometimes up to 4 m (13 ft) long—leads down to the den itself. At about 1–2 m (3–7 ft) wide by 1 m (3 ft) high, the sleeping chamber is usually not much bigger than the bear and is fitted with a clean "mattress" of grasses, moss and twigs for additional insulation and comfort. A bear may return in subsequent winters to the same den, or another other grizzly or even a black bear may claim an abandoned den.

In mountainous areas, grizzlies prefer to den on steep, north-facing alpine slopes or in subalpine terrain, at 1500–1800 m (4900–5900 ft) elevations, with deep snowfall for insulation. Toward the northern extent of the grizzly's range (mostly in the Yukon and Northwest Territories), south-facing slopes close to treeline are more favoured denning sites, and barren-ground grizzlies may move south to the treeline if they cannot find or dig out suitable dens on the tundra. The Richards Island grizzlies on the Tuktoyaktuk Peninsula den in the steep banks of rivers or lakes.

Depending on the location, elevation and climate, grizzly bears den for 3–7 months. In the south, grizzlies enter their dens by December, not leaving them again until late March or April. In northern climes, they may enter their dens as early as mid-October and emerge as late as May. They may not remain in the same den throughout that period, however. During their winter dormancy, during which the body temperatures of grizzlies do not fall by more than about 5° C (9° F), the animals can still be easily roused. Grizzlies dissatisfied with their current lodgings have been known to excavate a second den and move into new digs in midwinter. While denning, grizzlies do not eat or expel body wastes, and during this period they can lose up to 40 percent of their body weight.

A pregnant female enters her winter den to give birth to 1–4 (usually 2) cubs between the end of January and early March. She will stay in the den later in spring than males and nonnursing females, until her cubs, born completely dependent on their mother and weighing only about 500 g (18 oz), have achieved weights of about 3–4 kg (6.5–9 lb). Typically, a female reproduces every 3–5 years and remains with her young for 1.5–3.5 years. A mother grizzly with cubs can be roused from a den if disturbed, or she may venture out of her den to investigate after several days of unusually warm weather; the family may continue to use the den, staying in its vicinity in spring after they have technically left hibernation.

Female grizzlies are not sexually mature until 6–7 years of age. Males may become sexually mature sooner but likely cannot compete with established older males until they have some age to add body mass, strength and experience. Mating season is between late May and early July (later in northerly areas), but the implantation of the embryo is delayed until late fall, around the time the female enters her winter den. Grizzlies are polygamous, and cubs within a single litter may have different fathers. Cubs are weaned from their mothers in their second summer, and the female may not breed again until the following spring or even the spring after that.

Unlike black bears, grizzlies emerging from their dens have never been known to prey upon people. Instead, they seek out carrion from the winter kills of other animals or avalanches, young ungulates and the new shoots of plants. Nevertheless, they can still be dangerous if a person comes too close, especially if a bear is with cubs. Know how to identify a grizzly den, and avoid it if you see one.

UNDERSTANDING THE MOTIVATIONS AND DANGERS

As with all bears, the motivations leading to various behavioural responses are governed by the age, sex, health, vulnerabilities and hierarchical status of any given grizzly. Grizzly bears avoid people with much more determination than polar bears and black bears, which are respectively more curious by nature and more easily habituated. Grizzly bears do not tolerate any threat and strive to be at the top of their social ladder. They have no true predators other than other bears and humans.

Black bears avoid the larger and stronger grizzly bears by selecting different habitats, typically with trees that they can climb and grizzlies cannot. Quite possibly because they are used to deferring to their more powerful cousins, black bears can often be deterred by humans that they perceive to also present a risk. For grizzlies, which are not accustomed to yielding, the opposite is true, and they should never be threatened in any way.

If a grizzly detects another bear or a person, it reacts with aggression or avoidance. Hierarchy is recognized among male grizzlies and, especially during breeding season, a dominant male act will aggressively toward a subordinate. A young male in this situation knows that he does not have a chance and will likely retreat, whereas a sexually mature young male may try to fight the established bear to win dominance and breeding rights. A male bear that encounters a human at close range will also perceive the person to be a threat or a challenge and will assert its dominance by attacking.

A female tolerates other females, and females have not been shown to be hierarchical. A female without cubs that is interested in breeding with an approaching male behaves passively toward him. However, a female with cubs avoids male grizzlies, which may kill the cubs. When a female can't retreat from a bear—or human—that she perceives as threatening, her extremely strong protective instincts may provoke her to attack, and a marauding male may well be the one to retreat from a tough female!

Grizzly bears encountering members of their own species first communicate through posturing and vocalizations; if contact occurs, it almost always results in serious injury or death.

Grizzlies learn from experience, which explains why they remember positive experiences such as food reward and become conditioned so easily. They are in general opportunistic (governed by their appetites) but risk averse (grizzlies are very sensitive to human encroachment, which is why their status is vulnerable, and prefer to avoid people unless they become habituated and stop perceiving them as a threat). Grizzlies that have had bad experiences associated with humans learn to avoid people, which is why conservation officers have been successful with "intensive bear shepherding" using hazing methods and Karelian bear dogs. But, because you won't know the history of any given bear you happen to encounter, and because a grizzly encountering a human at close range is likely to perceive the intruder as a threat to its dominance, its food source or its cubs and become very hostile, it is important to treat grizzlies with respect and deference whenever possible.

Defensive Behaviour

If a grizzly is in a defensive situation, an attack is likely imminent if not immediate. If the bear does not react to your presence immediately with an attack, it may provide warnings through vocalizations, such as huffing, snorting, woofing, clacking its jaws, growling or showing its teeth, or posturing, such as pacing, swinging its head with its ears laid back or slapping the ground or a tree. *Make every effort to back away and remove yourself as a threat to the bear.*

A **female with cubs** is extremely protective, perhaps because she knows that only one in three cubs will survive the year even with her help. If you do not see cubs but encounter an extremely hostile grizzly, it is almost certainly defending either cubs or a food source. If you encounter cubs, ensure that you do not come between them and their mother. Even if you see cubs but no mother, she is likely nearby. Never intentionally approach the cubs or linger to take their photo unless you are at least 100 m (110 yd) away from both them and their mother.

A **grizzly defending a carcass or other food source** (which may not be visible) may give you warning to leave the area by the postures and vocalizations described above and may even make bluff charges. The hostile bear is encouraging you to leave the area.

Surprising a grizzly with your sudden appearance, not giving a grizzly sufficient time to avoid you or making it feel cornered will cause an aggressive reaction.

Offensive Behaviour

Offensive, or nondefensive, behaviour is more typical of black bears than grizzlies. Although offensive behaviour may be difficult to identify, an offensive bear shows little or no stress, aggression or agitation. It approaches deliberately, without the vocal or visual cues associated with defensive behaviour. In grizzlies, this behaviour is most likely to be observed in a young bear that is curious or habituated. Very rarely, a nutritionally stressed bear that is either food conditioned or habituated to human encounters in some way may act offensively. The bear is anticipating that you will get out of its way. Do not threaten this bear in any way that would encourage it to change its behaviour from benignly offensive to aggressively defensive. *Remain calm and quiet, watching the bear until it moves a respectable distance away—at least 100 m (110 yd).*

A **curious bear** may be a young individual assessing the situation at close range. At a distance, it may be a grizzly of any age or sex that has perhaps caught a scent that is unfamiliar or not yet identified. The bear will typically stand on its hind legs and sniff the air.

A **habituated bear** does not try to avoid human presence, either ignoring it or investigating it. Grizzly bears have been observed to walk directly past a campsite, seemingly ignoring it, and then just continue to amble about their own business. This behaviour is not an invitation to stay in the area. Once the bear moves on, move your camp and notify other campers as well as wildlife authorities of the sighting.

A **young and inexperienced habituated bear** may test its dominance with humans much as it would with other bears—by assuming postures and approaching to see if the person yields or challenges it. The bear may simply want to pass where a person is somehow blocking its route and expects or desires that the person move out of its path.

Another level of habituation is when the bear has a history of connecting human presence with a food source. A specific form of habituation involves the bear becoming **food conditioned**.

Predatory Behaviour

Predatory behaviour of grizzlies toward humans has never been proven to occur.

ENCOUNTERS

- if you see a grizzly bear
  - **stay calm and assess the situation**
  - do not approach the bear
- if the bear is unaware of you
  - move away quickly, calmly and quietly, keeping your eye on the bear
  - don't announce your presence to a bear that has not seen you and is over 100 m (110 yd) away
  - stay downwind and leave the area while keeping watch to see whether the bear notices you and follows
- if the bear is aware of you but does not advance
  - do not run away; a flight response may excite the bear or stimulate its instinct to chase you, and grizzlies have been recorded running up to 56 km/h (35 mph), which is much faster than even the world's fastest human runner
    - running downhill to evade a grizzly is a myth; grizzlies have no trouble running downhill
  - keep your eye on the bear but do not make direct eye contact, which may be perceived as threatening
  - raise your arms above your head to look larger

- o speak calmly to identify yourself as human
- o back away slowly or detour upwind to allow the bear to get your scent
- if the bear is aware of you and advances
- o remain facing the bear
- o speak to it in firm, low tones
- o back or move laterally out of the bear's path
- o if you are near a building or car
- ⊙ back toward it and get inside
- o if you do not have a car, building or safe area to retreat to
- ⊙ find a tree or large rock that may protect you
- ⊙ move uphill or elevate yourself onto a log or rock
- ⊙ raise your arms to look taller
- ⊙ do not enter a water body as solace from an attacking grizzly; this animal is an excellent swimmer
- o if you climb a tree
- ⊙ make sure you climb higher than 4 m (13 ft); grizzlies, although not as great climbers as black bears, can usually climb or reach to this height—but remember that one grizzly was documented to climb 15 m (50 ft) after its victim (see story, p. 92)
- ⊙ climb high enough that the branches are too small to support the bear's weight
- o if you are with other people
- ⊙ stay together and act as a group to deter the bear
- ⊙ make sure the bear has a clear escape route
- o as you back away, throw things *in front* of the bear as a distraction
- ⊙ a piece of clothing or a shoe is a good choice of something to throw
- ⊙ do NOT throw food in front of the bear, which will then recognize you as the source; if you have food with you, throw it far away from both you and the bear (off to the side, not between you and the bear or in the direction of your escape)

- ⊙ throwing down your backpack is debateable—definitely drop it if there is food in it; otherwise, if it's large, dropping it may create a distraction of sufficient interest to buy you time to find a shelter or leave the area, but wearing it can offer some protection to your back if you are attacked
- ⊙ do not throw anything directly at a bear, or you may provoke an attack
- if the bear continues to advance
  - o if you are carrying bear spray
  - ⊙ get it in your hand, point the nozzle away from you and check the wind direction to make sure the spray will not blow back on you
  - ⊙ use bear spray only if the bear comes within close range; within 1 m (3 ft) is optimal, but 3–4 m (10–13 ft) at most (see Bear Spray, p. 201)
  - ⊙ do not use bear spray if the bear is upwind
- if the bear charges
  - o a bluff charge is most likely; stand your ground but avoid eye contact (second-year cubs may participate with their mother in bluff charges); do not run or turn your back
  - o in a bluff charge, the bear stops short of contacting you and then begins to back away—at this point, you should also back away
  - o if the bear makes additional bluff charges
  - ⊙ continue to hold your stance during the charge
  - ⊙ continue to back away after the charge until the bear is sufficiently secure that you are retreating
- if the bear attacks
  - o play dead
  - ⊙ if you are carrying a backpack, keep it on your back for protection
  - ⊙ fall to the ground immediately and lie on your stomach, hands linked behind your neck and legs slightly splayed to give you leverage into the ground

to make it harder for the bear to flip you, OR roll yourself into a ball with your face tucked between your knees and your arms wrapped around them; grizzlies tend to attack the face and head, but be sure to protect your vital organs

⊙ if the bear does flip you over, return to your protective position and continue to play dead

o if the bear backs off

⊙ do not move or make a sound until you are sure the bear has left; moving or making noise while the bear is still within range may cause it to resume the attack because it still feels threatened

Note: When confronted with an aggressive grizzly during a *daytime* encounter, some experts recommend that you assume a passive position *before* the bear makes contact to assure the bear that you pose no threat to it.

BEAR 99

At four years old and a healthy 90 kg (200 lb), this bear, which would soon be tagged and known as Bear 99, had been an independent young grizzly since parting ways with his mother two years prior. At that time, he had begun exploring his world on the eastern slopes of the Rocky Mountains in Alberta. The rolling foothills of this region are more biodiverse than the mountain ranges themselves, with the lower elevations providing important migratory corridors and wintering grounds for wide-ranging species as well as having specific climatic and ecologic conditions well suited to numerous plants and animals.

People also like this scenic area. It has attracted people beginning with the First Nations and continuing with the arrival of the early settlers. It became even more popular in recent years with movies such as *A River Runs Through It*, after which people flocked to buy homes there. Property values soared, and local communities boomed with the development of some of the most elite houses and ranches in the country. Resort golf courses and mountain chalets began expanding into prime wildlife habitat.

As this boom began to take hold, environmentalists started demanding the mapping and protection of wildlife corridors on the eastern slopes. The Bow Valley Naturalists are working with the Alberta Government to keep people off a corridor a mere 300 m (330 yd) wide, but the proposition is being met with resistance from recreational users. The main town in this area of the foothills is Canmore, a community of 13,000 set between the busy city of Calgary 103 km (64 mi) to the east and the recreational playground of Banff National Park 3 km (2 mi) to the west, with the Trans-Canada Highway connecting them. It is in this mayhem of residential and recreational areas, campgrounds, ranches and lots of traffic that young Bear 99 was establishing his home range.

Grizzly and black bears, cougars and wolves—almost all the large predators—as well as fox, elk, deer and other Rocky

Mountain mammals must find their niche here among the human presence. All-terrain vehicles, which are not permitted in the national park, rip and tear across the delicate montane environs of the Eastern Slopes. With the advent of mountain biking, a proliferation of informal trails, approximately 200 km (125 mi) worth, further fracture the landscape. Bear 99 was attempting to find his own way through this maze.

Perhaps it was his personality that got him into trouble, or perhaps it was that he lived in an area where there were so many people who had never shown him any threat. Regardless, this particular grizzly became more and more curious about humans and less and less wary of avoiding them. Maybe he was also starting to establish his dominance and was not discriminating between his own species and humans in establishing that dominance.

The first time Bear 99 behaved inappropriately was on May 27, 2005, when he sauntered onto the fifth fairway of Canmore's Silvertip Golf Course, where grizzlies are a frequently observed golfing handicap. The bear then wandered east into the upper Cougar Creek residential area.

He soon encountered Niki Davison, a Canmore resident who was photographing wildflowers not far from her home. Although he seemed interested in following Niki and her basset hound, he did not attack. After about 10 minutes, he parted ways with the woman and her dog. The incident was, nonetheless, completely terrifying for her. "I heard something crashing behind me; when I looked up, I realized it was a grizzly," Niki stated to CBC TV reporters after the event. "When I realized it was a bear, it was kind of like your nightmare come true. I gathered my things and grabbed my dog and just backed up slowly."

Alberta Sustainable Resource Development Fish and Wildlife officers soon came to the area and set bear traps, which captured Bear 99 in short order. He was then shot with a tranquilizer gun and fitted with a radio collar before being flown by helicopter to the Carrot Creek area, just inside of the east boundary of Banff National Park. He was still within his home range area, only 15 km (9 mi) from where he was taken.

As Donna Babchishin, spokesperson at the time for the Alberta Sustainable Resource Development, explained in press reports, bears found behaving inappropriately that do not have a record of previous aggressive behaviour are commonly relocated within their home range; the relocation is mainly a deterrent to the bear. We can only guess as to what animals may experience during or remember after these experiences. Surely they must recognize at the time of being darted that they are being followed or attacked in some manner by humans. They feel the dart hit and then feel themselves lose consciousness.

So, when Bear 99 awoke, not in the same place from where he had lost consciousness, feeling probably a bit ill from the drugs and now wearing a rather large chunk of less-than-forest-fashionable jewellery around his neck, he should have made a negative association with humans and avoided them from then on at all costs. Unfortunately, that is not what happened.

Bear 99 was radio-collared for a reason: to observe his patterns of movement. When he started heading in the direction of Canmore within days, conservation officers began carefully monitoring his location. The early hours of June 4 were rainy, and Bear 99 was observed hunkering down in a shelter. Later, when the rain stopped, he wandered onto a ranch, where the rancher observed him and later commented that the young grizzly was easily scared off when he heard human voices. Bear 99 was showing typical behaviour with no cause for concern, but he was still being monitored. If necessary, the Fish and Wildlife officials had a Karelian bear dog (see Bear Dogs, p. 208) with which to haze the bear. Hazing is a technique to deter a bear from future encounters with people by exposing it to an unpleasant experience that it can remember as being associated with humans. The barking and harassment of one or two properly trained bear dogs is often adequate, but deterrents such as firecrackers and nonlethal projectiles such as rubber bullets or shot are also sometimes used.

On June 5 at about 9:30 AM, Bear 99 wandered back onto the Silvertip Golf Course, this time onto the 18th green. The maintenance crew scared him off and up into the treeline above the course.

It was later that same Sunday that Isabelle Dubé, age 36, was running with two other women in close proximity to the golf course on a trail known as the Bench Trail. Isabelle, a competitive mountain biker from Cap-St-Ignace (near Québec City), had competed in the TransRockies Challenge and was well known in the cycling community. On this occasion, she was doing some cross-training with her racing companion, Maria Hawkins, and another runner, Jean McAllister, when they were attacked by the bear at about 2 PM.

The inherent danger of being in a wildlife area is the extremely rare, but nevertheless possible, chance of a life-threatening wildlife encounter. Both Canadian and American parks authorities have made increasing efforts to educate the public on how to behave on a mountain trail in order to avoid, as much as possible, these kinds of encounters—especially with bears. One of the most important guidelines is to make yourself known by making enough noise to avoid surprising a bear. By following this rule, you reduce the chance of turning a corner and suddenly coming face-to-face with a grizzly, which has very strict comfort zones that people should never enter. Trail running is a particularly risky activity because the runner moves into a territory quickly and often quietly. This is what happened to Isabelle and her two friends, Maria and Jean, when they literally ran up to within a few metres of Bear 99.

As Maria and Jean later recalled in their public statement, "We encountered a grizzly bear; we stayed together and backed away from the bear. The bear came toward us like he was stalking us. He was not afraid." Each of the women made an immediate decision as to how to retreat from the advancing bear, they explained. "I.D. was a climber, and her instinct was to climb a tree," Jean continued. The bear followed Dubé's lead, leaving the other two women the window of opportunity to depart from the area without being followed by the bear. "Maria and I stayed together and continued to back away. We went for help," Jean was quoted as saying on Canada.com.

According to park and government authorities, the Bench Trail, across the lower slopes of Mount Lady MacDonald, had been closed to public use since April to protect a migratory corridor along the Bow River designed to allow wildlife, including cougars and bears, to move between areas of suitable habitat. The problem was that the Bench area is riddled with unofficial mountain-bike trails with over a dozen different ways to get in, many unmarked. The trail that the three women had selected as their way in was not marked as closed, so they probably would not have known to avoid the area.

The trail closure issue aside, the three women were appropriately running as a group rather than by themselves, and it was determined that they did everything correctly during the incident. Isabelle climbed up a tree as the two other women fled the scene to get help at the golf course. It is likely that the other two women escaped because Isabelle's climbing attracted more attention.

Unfortunately, Bear 99 was a stronger-than-average climber for his species and climbed after Isabelle. He pursued her 15 m (50 ft) up into the tree, which is 6 m (20 ft) higher than the average grizzly is known to climb, and dragged her down to the ground. By the time the other two women returned with help, Isabelle Dubé was dead, leaving behind a husband and young daughter.

Wildlife officers shot Bear 99 at the scene.

FEMALE WITH CUBS

One of the most dangerous and difficult-to-deter types of bear confrontations is one involving a female grizzly with cubs. According to the reports of people who have survived such attacks, which are based solely in defensive behaviour, playing dead has proven to be the only survival strategy.

One example dates from July 1992, when a cyclist in Jasper National Park came upon a female with cubs at too-close range. Likely as a consequence of the speed and relative silence of travel by bicycle, the bears did not have sufficient warning to avoid the encounter. Upon feeling threatened by the man's sudden appearance, the female attacked. He survived the attack by lying on the ground, covering his head and neck and enduring the onslaught until the female moved off. He was then able to flee the area and find help. (*Note:* if possible, use your bike as a shield between you and the bear; see Mountain Bike Safety, p. 177.)

*   *   *

Two hikers in Waterton Lakes National Park in September 1983 had everything going against them: they accidentally surprised a female with cubs that was defending a carcass. It is almost unbelievable how many bad stars were aligned for this situation to occur, and it is even more amazing that the victims survived.

According to their statements at the time, the couple had approached from downwind, and, when they saw the female bear, they were already within 15 m (50 ft) of her. They had not given her the chance to hear or smell them in time to avoid an encounter. As a result, she was startled and had both cubs and a bighorn sheep carcass to defend! The two hikers did not know at the time that there were cubs and a carcass, though; they saw only the female grizzly, which immediately charged. She went after the man first, as he was closest, while the woman tried to climb a tree.

The man lay facedown on the ground, keeping his pack on his back, and did his best to protect his head and neck with his hands. After inflicting significant injury, the bear moved on to the woman, who had managed to make her way a short distance up the tree. However, she lost her footing during the climb and fell to the ground, where she was also attacked. She claims to have tried not to resist, but at some point, she grabbed the bear's nose and twisted it.

Apparently, the bear was taken aback and turned back to attack the man once again. After a short but serious repeat performance, the bear turned away for good and left the two hikers where they lay. Mere minutes later, two other hikers arrived at the scene and ushered the two victims to medical attention. The bear and her as-yet-unseen cubs had apparently left the area.

Stephen Herrero discusses this case in his book *Bear Attacks* from his perspective as one of the wardens who returned to investigate the scene at the time. Acting with proper caution, he and his colleagues were quick to see the tracks of several grizzlies and determined that a female with cubs had made them. After they had been on the scene for some time, the wardens found the bighorn sheep carcass. At that point, they were going to leave and close the area to the public; however, the family of bears returned before they could depart. When the female saw the men, she again attacked. They had little choice but to shoot her.

*   *   *

The preceding two cases took place within national parks. A more recent case in September 2005 ended tragically in a remote area about 100 km (60 mi) southeast of Prince George, BC. Arthur Louie, a 60-year-old resident of Invermere, was driving on the Bowron River Service Road in a remote area between Prince George and the world-renowned Bowron Lakes Provincial Park when his car got a flat tire. Not far from the mining camp where he was stationed at the time, he began walking back. Nobody knows what happened, but Arthur's body was found in the bush 7 km (4 mi) from his abandoned truck. Conservation officers called in to investigate observed two young grizzly cubs only about 400 m (440 yd) from where he was discovered. The assumption was that the mother bear was somehow surprised by Arthur's presence, and that she attacked and killed him.

*　　*　　*

In April 2006, near Ross River, Yukon, a 28-year-old man was attacked by a female grizzly while staking a mineral claim for a mining company when he inadvertently walked too close to her den, where she was nursing her two three-month-old cubs; the man died from his injuries while awaiting rescue, and all three bears were destroyed."

*　　*　　*

In the following 1999 incident in the Yukon, Chris Widrig survived a violent attack that took his vision in one eye and nearly his life. Afterward, taking personal responsibility for the attack on him, he pleaded for the mother bear not to be destroyed as per the usual procedure. His appeal for the bear's life was supported by the remote location in which it occurred and the slim likelihood that another person would encounter the same bear under similar circumstances.

The attack took place in the vicinity of Goz Lake (near the Snake River), where Chris still owns and operates his own outfitting company, Widrig Outfitters (97) Ltd. He had purchased his own outfitting concession in this remote corner of the Yukon in 1986, 13 years after earning his original guide licence at the age of 18. Growing up in the mountain wilderness of BC, he began work in the mountains as a horse wrangler at age 14. By 1999, he was an experienced outdoorsman and hunter, was certified as a bush pilot and had seen many bears—among other fantastic wildlife—over the years.

Prior to the attack, the group that Chris was guiding had already seen one other female grizzly with a cub of the year. They saw her when they were still about 90 m (295 ft) away; they gave her a wide berth and continued past without incident. The relatively large size of the group and the respectable distance gave assurance to their confidence that the bear would prefer to avoid confrontation.

Chris and a fellow guide were leading four clients (two husband-and-wife couples) hunting Dall sheep. They travelled with 11 horses in a pack string. Everyone but Chris was riding—his horse was needed as an extra pack animal. On the day of the attack, August 9, they were over a week into the trip and had covered nearly 115 km (70 mi), with 80 km (50 mi) to go before arriving back at the base camp. The group had enjoyed sunny skies and warm weather throughout the trip so far, but on this day it started to rain. The ground was getting soggy, and the group decided they should find a good spot to set up camp for the night.

Chris was walking about 90 m (295 ft) ahead of the group along a well-defined trail through waist-high willow when he heard a loud "woof!" from somewhere behind him. He turned his attention in the direction of the noise and saw a female grizzly standing on her hind legs peering over the willows at him. Beside her was her second-year cub. They were only about 30 paces away.

Chris realized immediately that he was already too close. Worse, he had actually passed the bear and was now positioned with the bears standing between him and his group. He was not carrying a rifle—all he could do was yell "BEAR!" back to the others. And then he ran, which he would soon realize was a grave mistake. He looked back over his shoulder and saw that in those first few seconds the bears had not moved location, but the female had dropped back down onto all fours and kept looking between Chris and her cub. The horses by then had also seen the bears and had been spooked, with several taking off back up the trail. The hunters were frantically trying to grab their rifles from their scabbards. Chris, still running, soon looked back again, and this time the female grizzly growled, slapped the ground and then bolted in a full charge straight for him.

The next time Chris glanced back, the bear was hot on his heels and gaining; with the bear perhaps only 9 m (30 ft) away, he turned to face her and yell. This action had a momentary effect as the bear veered to one side, but she continued snapping her teeth and staring at him. Then she launched onto him, rearing up onto her hind legs and wrapping her massive forelegs around him in a deadly bearhug.

Chris remembers seeing her wide, gaping maw full of deadly teeth and smelling her foul breath before she bit into his face. Bite after bite tore away at his face and hands, and he could hear the bones of his skull cracking and the bones in his hands snapping "like chicken wings." Some victims of bear maulings recall not feeling the pain during the attack because of the effect of shock, but Chris was unfortunate enough to remain fully cognitive of the excruciating pain being inflicted with each bite.

Man and bear fell to the ground, Chris onto his back and the bear on top of him, continuing her attack. He managed to roll onto his stomach, and his heavy Gortex rainjacket was reasonably protective, considering that it was never designed to withstand bear molestations—the fabric seemed to bunch up and slip against the bear's teeth, and the man sustained only a very few puncture wounds to his back. But then she managed to flip him over again onto his back.

By this time his face was so damaged that he could no longer open his eyes. He could only feel the continuing assault, hear the roaring and smell the bear's hot, rancid breath. The bear redirected its attack onto Chris's legs, swiping at them with her great claws, causing a 23-cm (9-in) gash on his inner right thigh just shy of his femoral artery. Then, less than two minutes after the dramatic attack began, it was over with the first shot from one of the hunter's rifles. Although she was not hit, the bear bolted immediately back into the bush.

The group ran to Chris's side and did their best to tend to his injuries, but the packhorses had run off with all the emergency supplies. Two members of the group turned to retrieve them while the others stayed with Chris. They took Chris's wet clothing off him while one of the men stripped down to donate his warm, dry gear. Then they waited for two hours for the return of the other two with the packhorses and supplies. It was by now windy and rainy, with one man semi-naked and another critically injured.

At last the horses were returned, and the group quickly set up tents and sleeping bags and administered whatever first aid they could to Chris's wounds. He was still unable to see and was bleeding and shivering from the shock and cold. Two of the more skilled riders took four of the horses and rode the 80 km (50 mi) to base camp and help. They took the GPS reading of their coordinates to relay to the rescue helicopter that would be called in.

The attack had occurred at 1 PM. It took two more hours to catch the spooked horses, another hour to set up camp and make sure Chris was sheltered and his wounds were being attended, and then there was the long ride for help. Although the two riders made excellent time and arrived at the base camp in 14 hours, it was 6 AM the following day before help could be summoned. Were such an attack to occur today, they would have been able to carry a PLB to summon an immediate emergency search-and-rescue response without the 17-hour delay (see PLB information on pp. 12 & 214–15). At the time, these devices were not widely available and were very heavy and expensive. Chris was carrying a satellite radio but was unable to gain reception.

The people who remained with Chris kept him awake through the night, talking to him and reassuring him that he would be fine and preventing him from going into shock. By 9 AM, battling stormy weather, the helicopter arrived with a doctor, nurse and morphine. He was flown immediately to Whitehorse, where, coincidentally, an opthalmologist was in town on his once-per-month visit and examined Chris's eyes. Significant damage to the tear ducts, orbital lobes and retinas—in addition to all the other facial injuries that would require reconstructive plastic surgery—made it necessary to medevac him to Vancouver, where he arrived by 11 PM.

Thirty-six hours after the attack, Chris went into emergency surgery. However, even suffering through 200 stitches, metal plates and the loss of sight in one eye was not enough for Chris to harbour thoughts of revenge against the bear. When the conservation officer heading out to investigate the attack site said to Chris that protocol dictates that the bear be destroyed, Chris responded by saying explicitly that he did not want that bear to be shot, noting that "it would be totally pointless to kill her; she was just defending her cub. She may never see another person again." The plea was heard, and the bear was spared.

In retrospect, Chris realizes that it was his incautiously walking too far from the group and lack of access to a rifle that led to the incident, and he explains that running away and making eye contact with the bear were both likely erroneous actions. His first error provoked the mother bear into attack mode, and his second would have caused her to perceive him as a definite threat. However, by not fighting back once the attack ensued (because he was up against a grizzly and not a black bear), he likely reduced the amount of damage. In his defence, only when you are in the position of being attacked by a full-grown and very angry grizzly can you really know how you yourself would react, and a lot of what happens is governed by instinct and panic.

Once he recovered, Chris returned to work and published his story in his 2004 book, *Of Man and Beast*. Within this publication he acknowledges the potential perils of his chosen livelihood: "In our profession we should expect to occasionally face a bear attack, a charging bull moose in the rut, a drowning accident when crossing a river, or crashing with an aircraft. These are risks I take by being an outfitter."

FISHING AND HUNTING IN GRIZZLY BEAR COUNTRY

The solace in nature attracts many of us to spend time alone in wilderness areas to "get away from it all," to find silence for quiet contemplation. Some people may find the sport of fishing meditative, whereas others find hunting a way to feel part of nature, part of a balance and connection with the natural order. When in these moments of tranquility or in the practice of the stalk, the last thing one wants to do is start making a lot of noise. However, making noise is one of the primary recommendations for warding off the possibility of a bear encounter.

Because they are, understandably, reluctant to make noise, because their recent and cached kills are often readily claimed by opportunistic nearby bears and because they are more likely to visit remote areas, hunters are more likely than any other category of wilderness user group to have hostile encounters with bears. For many of the same reasons, anglers, taken as a group, are also at high risk.

Several cases in Canada illustrate the various situations in which anglers and hunters may come into dangerous contact with a grizzly. Within the past decade, one man trout fishing alone along the South Castle River in southwestern Alberta was killed by a grizzly (August 1998), and two hunters were mauled by a grizzly they accidentally snuck up on while hunting (June 1999).

Then there is the case is of Harvey Cardinal, a hunting guide who was killed by a grizzly in 1970 near Fort St. John, BC, which was unusual in that it took place in mid-January, a time of year when bears are typically in their winter dens.

The danger of having a grizzly claim a carcass of a hunting kill is very real. Another hunting guide was mauled back in 1968 near Grande Cache, Alberta, by a grizzly that claimed the carcasses of two moose that the hunters had shot. They had left the carcasses overnight and returned the next day to retrieve them without appropriate caution; they were within

11 m (35 ft) of the bear by the time they noticed it. The bear attacked and mauled the guide in defence of this food source. Then, in October 1995, near Radium Hot Springs, BC, two young men were dressing and quartering the carcass of a bull elk that they had killed when a sow grizzly and her two cubs came upon the men by surprise and killed the men to claim the carcass. The three bears were later shot by conservation officers.

The foregoing tragic examples demonstrate that you need to be especially wary when handling, moving or gutting a carcass, and that you should never try to reclaim a carcass from a grizzly (it is illegal to kill a bear that has taken over a game carcass). Hunt with at least one other person so that you can post a lookout with binoculars to watch for bears attracted to the smell of a carcass that is being handled. For the protection of other people in the area, report any gut piles you leave or find to local conservation or natural resources authorities (also see Hunting Safety, p. 178).

*   *   *

As of this writing, the most recent grizzly attack on a hunter in Canada took place on November 30, 2007, when 51-year-old Don Peters from Calgary was attacked and killed by grizzly while out hunting big game near Mountain Aire Lodge west of Sundre, 90 km (55 mi) northwest of Calgary. Peters was an avid hunter and knew how to conduct himself in the wilderness. The weather was very cold and snowy; conditions and time of year likely made Peters confident not to encounter a bear, which would normally have been in its winter den by this time. Nevertheless, bear behaviour remains to some degree unpredictable, the nature of the hunter is silent and his hunting grounds were remote, thereby setting the scene for a surprise encounter.

When Peters did not return to the lodge on Sunday, a search party was sent out, but it took three days to find him. An Alberta RCMP emergency response team, numerous Fish and Wildlife officers, members of the Alberta Sustainable Resource Development bear response team and a trained Karelian bear dog were brought to the scene to protect members of a voluntary search party of 20 men from the nearby hunting lodge (one in four of which carried a rifle).

Peters had been hunting in a heavily wooded area and had set up a blind in a stand of trees, behind which to hunt. Some distance away from the structure, 200 m (220 yd) from his vehicle, Peters was found dead. One shot had been fired from his rifle. Speculation is that perhaps he was searching for a different location for his blind or that he was checking something out in the woods. Searchers found a deer hidden nearby that may have been a grizzly cache that the man had stumbled upon. After Peters had been found, the search continued for what Fish and Wildlife officers now believed was a grizzly that killed Peters, but no blood trail or other sign that the bear had been wounded was found. The area was closed to the public while the search continued for several days, but the search was called off with the belief that the bear had gone into its winter den and would not be found.

The following spring (March 2008), a female bear was shot and positively identified as the bear that had killed Peters. Her two cubs, now a year old, were left to survive on their own.

*   *   *

Chris McLellan, 32, was lucky to survive to tell of his encounter with a grizzly while out reconnoitring possible bow-hunting sites on a mid-August day in 2007. Although he had moved to northwestern Alberta from Nova Scotia just days before, he had years of experience in the outdoors.

The encounter took place in a field of oats some 12 km (7.5 mi) south of Grovedale, which is itself about 21 km (13 mi) south of Grande Prairie. Chris was out late. Around 9:30 PM, just as the sun was setting, he accidentally walked right up to a female grizzly with three cubs. He had been moving quietly through the field and did not see the mother grizzly behind a knoll. She had obviously picked up on his scent and stood up on her hind legs, revealing herself to him at some 55 m (180 ft) away. He was wearing a camouflage mask at the time and later explained to reporters that he pulled off the mask and began yelling and waving his arms in hopes that the bear would then identify him as human and flee. Instead, she dropped to all fours and charged.

Chris had nowhere to run, so he held his ground, later recounting how the bear never slowed down but ran directly toward him, eyes focused upon him, huffing as she ran, clearly not intending a bluff charge. Remarkably, he maintained the presence of mind to attempt to deter the bear without injury by taking out his digital camera and switching it to night mode, hoping to use the flash to startle her and make her shy off.

The flash failed to fire, however, and the bear continued to advance, so Chris grabbed his 30-cm (12-in) hunting blade, held it above his head and braced himself for contact with the bear. She slammed into him, knocking him down in a manner that he compared to a football check. As the grizzly hit his torso, she seized his left arm with her teeth. At that very moment, he drove the knife blade fully into the base of her neck. Judging by the amount of blood that immediately sprayed over them both, it was apparently a lethal target, but the bear continued to pursue her attack, biting him in his midsection and then his knife arm. Nevertheless, he managed to plunge the knife into her neck two more times before his attacker turned away. Both animal and human retreated in opposite direction, Chris to the help of the farmer, who summoned medical help, and the bear to her death—her body was discovered the next day.

Chris told his tale from his hospital bed in Edmonton, where he was treated for broken bones and a partially severed nerve in his left forearm and wounds to his right arm and torso. Remaining calm under pressure likely saved his life, although the realization of how things could have been much worse came to him afterward, as he told reporters. He said that he hopes to heal well enough to be able to bow hunt again.

The foregoing is not simply a case of bad luck, being in the "wrong place at the wrong time," as is often the catch phrase with so many bear attacks. It is a case of wrong behaviour (not making noise while watching for game opportunities) at the wrong time (dusk) and the wrong place (a ripening oat field in grizzly territory, given that bears are partial to grain) that almost cost Chris McLellan his life and did cost the bear her life (the survival of her three cubs is unknown). Being new to the area, Chris likely did not realize the risk he was taking; had he done more research and taken all these factors into account, he could very well have avoided this unfortunate bear encounter.

BEARS AND DOGS

Late in the day on September 12, 2005, Christopher (13) and Mathew (15) Solecki and their dog Snowpup were walking the edge of the bush that runs along their family's 300-head cattle ranch in the Lakes District of the BC interior. The ranch is 30 km (20 mi) to the south of Burns Lake, one of the many lake communities in the district adjacent to BC's largest provincial park, Tweedsmuir Provincial Park. The boys were carrying bear spray because of the high number of black bears in the area, which they were used to seeing almost daily.

Although grizzlies were also known to visit the area, it was unusual to see them, and they were more of a concern during calving season in spring. For the most part, the bears were pretty shy of people—but maybe not so shy of dogs, as would soon become apparent.

Snowpup took off into the bush, into a swampy area, and was out of sight for less than a minute before he re-emerged with a large grizzly hot in pursuit. The dog ran straight toward the two boys, leading the bear right to them. Christopher was in the lead when Snowpup blazed past, so the grizzly redirected its grievances onto the next available target, knocking him down to the ground with a single blow to his legs before either boy had a chance to grab his bear spray.

They were still near the house, so Mathew turned back, yelling for his dad, who was working outside the house. Hearing the barking and screaming, he ran out to his sons. The bear was already gone, and his young son lay conscious but bleeding profusely from his head.

A 911 call was made, and soon a helicopter was transporting Christopher to the nearest hospital, where he was stabilized before being flown to BC Children's Hospital in Vancouver. Christopher had several bite punctures and scratches on his body and a fractured thighbone from when the grizzly had first made contact with him that required two pins, but more serious were a torn scalp and a severely fractured skull. The bone fragments puncturing the left side of his brain required seven hours of neurosurgery and several months of physical therapy. During his initial visit, he had to stay in the hospital under supervision for almost two weeks—a special concern with bear bites is the risk of bacterial infection in case the animal had been feeding on carrion. All together, it took many months and many surgeries to repair the damage.

Conservation officers investigating the incident concluded that the bear had been provoked by the dog, Snowpup. With the bear in pursuit, Snowpup ran back toward the boys and in doing so brought the bear into immediate contact with people that it otherwise would likely have avoided. Out of fear and anger, the grizzly lashed out at the boy that was suddenly directly in front of it. The bear's attack on Christopher ended quickly—the boys were only 300 m (330 yd) from their father, who ran out as soon as he heard their calls, and the bear was already gone when he arrived. The bear had no intention of preying on the boy and immediately fled the scene.

This story is an example of how taking a dog into bear country can cause a bear confrontation rather than prevent one. Dogs either have to be very well trained to stay walking with their owners, or they need to be restrained by a leash. Only a properly trained bear dog understands what behaviour to use in deterring a bear (see story, p. 165).

Unlike the untrained Snowpup, who ran off into the bush and came back with a bear in pursuit, thereby provoking an attack, Karelian dogs are bred for hunting predatory wildlife such as bears, wolves and cougars and are also specifically trained for use by conservation officers for dealing with problem bears. BC and Alberta conservation officers have begun to employ Karelian bear dogs. Originating from the Karelian region of Finland, they are bred and trained as hunting dogs. They will hunt any large game but are particularly noted for being quite fearless of bears. They will defend their owners at the cost of their own lives if necessary. Like most dogs bred for aggressive traits, they must be owned only by experienced dog handlers. The great success seen in the ability of Karelian bear dogs to shepherd bears and aversely condition them away from specific human-use areas such as campsites, garbage bins and residential areas may see more Karelians used by conservation officers and park wardens and perhaps supplant, at least in part, the former approach of relocating these nuisance bears.

There have been several cases reported of Canadians being saved by their faithful canine companions in the wake of a grizzly bear attack. In 1999 alone, there were four cases in BC where people reported aggressive grizzly bears that were deterred by their dogs, either distracting the bear while the people escaped or chasing the bear off. None of these dogs were killed, either. Whether the people under attack in these four cases were just lucky, or whether their dogs were under better control or were simply more savvy about bears is not known.

If you bring your dog with you when walking in bear country, it is always wise (and often legally required) to have your pet on a leash to avoid having it dash off into the bushes and perhaps provoke a bear. In the event of a bear encounter, holding the dog on the leash offers you more protection than if the dog is loose. Keeping the dog by your side may deter the bear, whereas allowing the dog to run around and bark at the bear may annoy it and agitate it further.

BEAR SPRAY

The effectiveness of bear (pepper) spray is demonstrated in this account from July 2007. At the time, two forestry contractors from Cranbrook, BC, were marking a cutblock near the White River. It was a hot, dry day. The man and woman were ribboning off the boundaries of a creek draw (a seasonally wet gulch) prior to the crews coming in to cut the trees. As the man walked from the thick vegetation into a clearing, he came face-to-face with a medium-sized, cinnamon-coloured grizzly, surprising both himself and the animal. The man yelled "bear!" to his coworker and then dove for cover.

Panicked and angered by this uninvited and unexpected invasion into its space, the startled grizzly charged to attack the intruder responsible for disrupting its day. Attempting to shield himself as best he could from the assault that was about to be inflicted upon him, the man wiggled himself deeply into the brush. The bear in turn rampaged through the brambles, biting and clawing at the man's arms and legs.

As the forestry worker kicked and flailed his appendages—half the time in avoidance and half the time in counter attack—he managed to land a solid kick dead square in contact with the bear's snout with one of his metal-spiked "cork" (caulk) boots, and the grizzly jumped back. Deterred from the man, the cranky bear now turned its attention to the coworker, who by this time had her pepper spray aimed and ready. When the bear came within 1.8 m (6 ft), she sprayed a strong blast directly into the bear's face. The bear was immediately heavily affected, coughing and wheezing and completely distracted from its previous concerns with the people. The woman gave the bear spray to her coworker and ran 4 km (2.5 mi) to obtain help from another crew, who then called for air ambulance and returned to help the man.

When help arrived, the bear had remained deterred—although quite likely still somewhere nearby—by the spray and had not returned to cause the man further injury. The injured man was airlifted to the hospital, where he was treated for puncture wounds and lacerations. Conservation officers who came to investigate the area of the attack reported no sign of cubs or that the bear had been feeding or defending a carcass. It was determined that the bear had been sleeping in the deep creek draw to avoid the heat of the midday sun. Unwittingly, the man had simply startled the bear, something that grizzlies do not tolerate.

WHEN RELOCATION DOESN'T WORK

Grizzlies and humans don't mix, and mutual avoidance is an instinctual survival and safety response in both species. The problem is that both grizzlies and humans appreciate the same wilderness areas—the grizzlies for habitat and the humans for recreation, industry, housing and agriculture. Canadians have been hearing from the media for years about the plight of sensitive species such as the grizzly but also including the cougar, wolf, martin, caribou, moose and many other charismatic species that are harmed by human impacts on their habitat. Many of these species suffer such encroachment on their habitat in silence, but bears are not so discreet and often become what we term "nuisance bears." For many years now, the response has been to either shoot or relocate such "problem" animals.

However, although relocation is preferable to shooting the bear, it should not be seen as a benign and simple solution. Relocation is not always successful because the bear may return. Also, it has the potential to be dangerous to the bear (risks include death from reaction to the sedative drugs, attack from a resident bear in the relocation area and not being able to adapt to unfamiliar territory or find new food sources) and dangerous to the people in charge of relocating the bear (for example, if it recovers too quickly from the drugs and attacks). Instead, it is preferable not to create nuisance bears in the first place.

Some people are quick to suggest that certain areas coveted for human use should see the bears managed rather than the people and that grizzlies are too dangerous to be in our space and should simply be relocated elsewhere in the abundant forests and wilderness areas for which Canada is famous. Consider that the Bow Valley of the eastern slopes of the Rocky Mountains—the key wildlife corridor and sparse montane habitat—is a mere 4 km (2.5 mi) wide. Within this narrow strip, humans have developed the national parks of Banff and Jasper for our recreational pleasures, complete with golf courses, ski resorts, an airstrip and hotels. The town of Banff and the village of Jasper have all the amenities of a city, and the Trans-Canada and 1A highways and a national railway cross the parks and are responsible for a great number of wildlife mortalities, including those of large carnivores.

But, what montane areas are we leaving for the bears? The estimated grizzly population in Banff is 50–100, and these bears must somehow cope with the approximately 4.5 million human tourists who visit the area each year. We have put our footprint throughout grizzly habitat, and we can no longer say that this part of the montane is for people whereas another is still intact for wildlife and is where grizzlies can simply be relocated. Outside of park boundaries, the foothills are scarred with coalmines, clearcuts and other intensive industrial practices as well as damage from activities such as driving off-road vehicles. Pristine wilderness areas no longer exist on the eastern slopes.

Bear No. 16, nicknamed Skoki, is an example of how the Bow Valley lost its attempt at hosting a grizzly. It had been several years since a grizzly had been able to tolerate the high human activity levels in this area, so when a juvenile grizzly made the effort in 1993, Parks Canada did not intervene and monitored both the bear and tourists to be able to mediate any inappropriate behaviours from either party. Skoki was temporarily immobilized and fitted with a radio collar so that he could be tracked. It was surmised that because this bear was a subadult just establishing his own home range, he had been pushed out of more "wild" areas containing the established territories of older, dominant grizzlies. In his wanderings, he had discovered the bountiful yields of buffaloberries growing alongside the Trans-Canada Highway that cuts through Banff National Park—an area most experienced grizzlies would try to avoid. Most of the grizzly mortality in the national parks of the Rocky Mountains, which is almost equivalent to the grizzly birth rate, is by road and rail accident. Skoki was in a precarious area that was only becoming more dangerous because

of the traffic backups caused by tourists stopping their cars along the highway to photograph the bear.

Conservation officers in Alberta have recognized that bear viewing and photographing invite habituation. In the words of District Fish and Wildlife Officer Kirk Olchowy of Blairmore, Alberta, "Watching or photographing bears at short ranges (under 200 m [220 yd]) for extended periods of time is likely just as irresponsible as leaving your garbage out in your campsite. These bears are learning the wrong message."

Extra work time by conservation officers in the park was required to police the tourists so they wouldn't stop on the highway, and aversive conditioning directed at Skoki by hazing was met with only limited success. The bear reacted with more aggression and a few bluff charges rather than retreating, and he continued to return to the site, implying that the aversive conditioning was not a sufficiently negative experience to have the desired effect. By the end of the berry season, however, Skoki left the roadside in search of other food sources and eventually went into his winter den.

With the arrival of spring, Skoki reacquainted himself with his newly established territory and, still wearing his radio collar, was observed roaming the Bow Valley in search of food. Spring passed without incident, but a large grain spill on the CP rail line in July 1994 attracted Skoki and five black bears to feed on the spill. Again, aversive conditioning to deter the bears from the area proved ineffective, and the area had to be closed off to human use because of the high public safety hazard from these bears defending their food source.

However, 1994 proved to be a good year for berry yields, and once the berries were in season, the bears moved off the grain spill back to natural food sources. Skoki was observed in the area between Baker Creek and Johnston Canyon, and after he passed through the campground a few times, signs were posted to warn the public of his presence in the area. By this time, as a result of the roadside "bear jams" of tourists, the conservation officers at the grain spill and the high densities of campers in the campgrounds (although he avoided any encounters), Skoki was becoming habituated to human presence.

In September 1994, Skoki stumbled upon an illegal back-country campsite near Castle Junction and didn't appreciate the intrusion into his space. After the bear made a bluff charge at the campers that was a little too close for comfort, they quickly vacated and reported their experience to park officials. The nearby hostel also reported an aggressive grizzly—it was Skoki. The wardens knew there was nothing left to do but capture the bear and decide what to do with him because he was no longer welcome in his home. The area was closed off from human use, and traps were set.

Capture was unsuccessful, so an intense aversive conditioning effort was implemented to relentlessly haze Skoki to encourage him to flee west away from the high human activity areas. It seemed to have worked when his signal was lost for a solid two weeks, after which he was caught in a bear snare set up for a bear study near the Lake Louise ski resort. He was sedated, had his collar replaced and was released onsite.

By mid-October, Skoki was back at the site of the grain spill. Although it had been significantly cleaned up by now, the bear managed to dig up enough buried grain along the tracks near the highway to keep him interested, leading to further traffic delays and public safety concerns. Under the watchful supervision of diligent wardens and conservation officers, he remained in this area until mid-November, when he finally moved off; telemetry data identified him entering a winter den somewhere between Castle Mountain and Protection Mountain.

Hopes were that by the following spring, which would be 1995, Skoki would be sexually mature and would expand his range into more remote areas in search of a mate. Unfortunately, such was not to be the case. After another year of intensive monitoring and public safety concerns, even though Skoki never harmed any of the hundreds of humans he encountered, the risk was too great; his increasing level of boldness was warning of the potential for human injury or death. He would no longer be permitted to roam in freedom. On July 5, 1996, this young, wild, healthy grizzly was captured and moved permanently into an enclosure at the Calgary Zoo.

Skoki was spared his life (although one might debate the relative quality of his life in captivity), but the loss of this bear from the Bow Valley ecosystem and from the genetic pool of the Eastern Slopes grizzly population is equivalent to the death of the bear. The latest studies on the Alberta population of grizzlies indicate it to be less than 500, perhaps as low as 400; any death or removal of a bear is significant, especially when the figure that has been targeted in the past decade for a sustainable grizzly bear population in Alberta is 1000 individuals.

As the above case study shows, a significant amount of effort is needed to protect both people and grizzlies from harming each other in the parks. However, even in a province as wealthy as Alberta, the costs of monitoring people (such as tourists uneducated as to how to deal with bear presence) and monitoring just one single bear on a daily basis are not deemed affordable.

A wildlife management approach that treats the symptoms rather than the underlying cause is unsustainable. Species such as the grizzly cannot survive in our mountain parks unless we implement strict controls on human densities in tourist areas and acknowledge what a protected area really is—with the growth of permanent urban settlement in the mountain parks, it is arguable whether the promise to protect wilderness in these national parks has been kept. In addition, we need to extend viable protected areas with mitigation against human impacts to allow for migration and habitat security for this far-ranging species and others.

*   *   *

With ample natural vegetation and strong spawning runs of all five Pacific salmon species, the Bella Coola Valley in BC is another prime habitat location for grizzly bears. The valley is home to an estimated 60 resident grizzlies, and 100 or more bears can be present at one time when factoring in new spring cubs or the fall influx of nearby nonresident grizzlies attracted to the salmon runs. Here again is an example of where high quality habitat has not gone unnoticed by humans. In this case, the highly productive flood plain of the valley made it desirable for agriculture, and today it sustains fruit orchards and livestock.

The highly productive forests nearby have been hard hit by clearcuts, pushing more wildlife into the valleys, as did the major forest fire of 2004 in Tweedsmuir Provincial Park. Tweedsmuir is known for its bear viewing opportunities, which some conservation officers and researchers have suggested is habituating the bears to human presence and potentially making them bolder around anglers. Is it fair to say that these grizzlies should be relocated elsewhere? Where else would equivalent habitat exist? Park staff are using rubber bullets for aversive conditioning to keep the bears wary, and the installation of electric fencing in 2004 at the Bella Coola landfill that attracted and habituated numerous grizzly bears had an impact. In just a few years prior to the fence being installed, conservation officers shot and killed 14 grizzlies thought to be conditioned to garbage and unlikely candidates for relocation.

*   *   *

An example of an unsuccessful relocation occurred in Lake Louise, when a female grizzly with two cubs attacked sleeping campers on November 25, 1995. The bears were reported to have gone on a "rampage," knocking down tents and attacking people. Six campers sustained injuries, some of them serious, but luckily, none of them fatal. Because their camp was clean, there is only speculation as to the cause of the attack. These bears had been recently relocated in the vicinity of Spray River after causing a nuisance in Revelstoke. The female with her two cubs and another female bear were getting into public garbage, destroying private property and making residents nervous of their presence. At the time, the relocation seemed the only solution for the problem that Revelstoke had created with its dump.

It is difficult to know where to relocate bears so as not to interfere with other bears' territories. The female bear and her two cubs were relocated to Spray River, which is not very far from Lake Louise, and not an unreasonable distance for a bear to travel in search of new food sources in what would now be unfamiliar territory for this mother who now needed to quickly discover food sources to feed her two hungry cubs. In the stress of learning an unknown territory and watching for the presence of male grizzlies that may threaten her cubs, she may have been reverting to learned behaviour in returning to a human food source in the heavily human-populated Lake Louise. In the way of her search, she found the sleeping campers. She and her two cubs were subsequently shot inside the national park.

Ironically, all the way back in 1938–39, a park-wide survey taken in the Bow Valley led to the superintendent listing specific areas as "known to be favoured" by grizzlies, and one such area was the Spray River Valley. Only after this incident with the female grizzly and her cubs was a report written suggesting that the Spray River Valley from Canyon Dam at Spray Lakes to Goat Creek be restricted from human access to protect grizzlies and wolves from human disturbance. If this restriction had been implemented earlier (say, some 60 years earlier), human injury and the death of those bears may have been prevented.

*   *   *

Relocation is risky for the bear, which is given a very strong drug and transported, then has to survive in unknown territory that is potentially already occupied by other grizzlies. Relocation is also risky for the researchers, who have to capture and handle the bear and ensure that it recovers from the drug, but not while they are handling the bear. This activity has put many researchers in very dangerous, sometimes fatal situations. Wilf Etherington was a biologist employed by the Canadian Wildlife Federation. Back in 1973, he and photographer Bill Schmaltz were helping with the relocation of a garbage-habituated grizzly in Banff National Park. This 239-kg (527-lb) bruin had been drugged and taken to a remote area of the park by a helicopter piloted by Jim Davies, who was very experienced at relocating grizzlies. Wilf and Bill were filming the grizzly for research purposes as it was recovering from the sedation.

Bill and Wilf were quite close to the released and apparently still-drugged animal when Jim decided to fly over the bear to assess the situation. The bear jumped up from its sleeping posture, showing little sign of being drugged, and charged the helicopter. Wilf and Bill continued to photograph this remarkable recovery by the bear and approached within 40 m (140 ft).

Jim was uncomfortable with the situation, so he landed the aircraft nearby and walked over to the two men to tell them to head back to the helicopter. However, just as he reached the two men, the bear charged at them. The three men reacted at first by backing away slowly but then made the quick decision to run for the helicopter. Jim was in the lead to get to the helicopter and start the engine, and he was followed close behind by Bill, but Wilf was falling behind. He dropped his pack hoping it would distract the bear, but it did not. The bear soon reached Wilf, knocked him down and began biting his face.

Jim and Bill had reached the helicopter and flew toward the bear that was still mauling Wilf. They managed to chase it off about 140 m (450 ft) down a hill, but they were too late—Wilf was dead. They left the scene and returned with park wardens and rifles. The body had not been moved. The bear was hiding in a nearby bushy area but charged at the helicopter as it circled. The bear was shot three times and killed.

The drug Sernylan, which had been used to tranquilize this bear, is no longer used for this purpose today because it is also sought after as a street drug, "angel dust." Sernylan has been observed to instil aggressive behaviour in human users, and, as this case demonstrates, it may have similar effects on bears.

Polar Bear

Ursus maritimus
ours polaire or *ours blanc* in French; *nanuq* in
  Inuktitut

Although the polar bear has a fearsome reputation, fewer than a dozen human mortalities caused by this species have been documented in the world. Accounts of killings by both the grizzly and black bear are far more numerous. According to researchers, the polar bear is less defensive and aggressive than the grizzly, and it is not easily agitated; more risk-averse, it tends to prefer to avoid confrontations.

In most encounters with humans, the polar bears were surprised, hungry or simply curious. Situations with predatory bears have tended to be specific to malnourished individuals, typically juveniles unskilled at hunting or old, sick or emaciated individuals no longer physically strong enough to hunt. Maulings have also occurred, but with a low frequency considering the number of human–polar bear encounters. Female polar bears almost never attack humans unless they are surprised or they are with cubs and humans approach too closely. The age-and-sex class most commonly involved in polar bear attacks is subadult males. These bears are generally not emaciated or desperate but—not unlike many human teenage boys—aggressive and inexperienced.

Most polar bear encounters are with local people who know how to conduct their behaviour and activities on the land to reduce the chance of meeting a bear but are prepared and know how to react if they do encounter one. Through generations of experience, traditional northern people—the Inuit and Innu—have learned how to avoid injury by polar bears for the most part. They have also traditionally hunted polar bears, so deterring them often simply meant shooting them. Today, the local people living and working, fishing and hunting in polar bear territory know how to deter a polar bear, and, if the polar bear cannot be deterred, they know how to defend themselves. In these human–polar bear encounters, polar bears are killed by people more often than people are killed by polar bears.

Most native communities in the Arctic are near the coastlines, largely along the shores of fiords, which is where the ice starts to form in October and where polar bears begin to congregate as they await the freeze-up of the water. Most of the human population in Nunavut lives in the Baffin (Qikiqtaaluk)

region, which is where an estimated 62 percent or more of Nunavut's polar bear population also lives. Greater land use by people, such as increased residential populations or tourism in some areas or more industrial development in others, increases the rate of human-bear interaction, either habituating or stressing bears in the vicinity.

In this region, most bears are killed in defence of life or property during the open-water season, from late summer through to the start of winter, when the bears are on land. September is the month with the minimum amount of sea ice. When freeze-up occurs, the bears move onto the ice to hunt marine prey, primarily seals. A late freeze-up increases the amount of time that polar bears remain on the coast as they await the ice-hunting season and thereby increases the rate of human-bear conflict with nearby communities. By January or February, human–polar bear conflict in the Baffin region is rare.

Yet, in other areas of the North—notably the Beaufort Sea area, where people work on oil rigs, seismic studies or environmental studies—the ice pack retreats offshore in the summer months. The bears return with the ice in winter, and it is then that they are in proximity to humans. There were several human–polar bear incidents in the 1970s, when exploration and development along the Beaufort Sea was just beginning and most intensive. A few of those resulted in human death, but there have been no further fatalities since those early days.

During the 25–30 years of a polar bear's life (captive individuals have lived over 40 years), the animal follows a well-defined calendar of activities. As a result, human-bear encounters are more likely at certain times of year, and these encounters are more likely to be dangerous at specific times. Although the ecology of polar bears is fairly complex, knowing when and where these bears den, hunt, breed and roam suggests when you are likely to find them in the areas where these activities take place.

Trying to understand the motivations and activities of these great bears can reduce the chance of an encounter. However, every individual bear is as unpredictable as every individual person, and being in the wilderness is, indeed, a wild experience. The few accounts in this chapter illustrate how rare fatal polar bear attacks really are—only five have been recorded in Canada in the past half-century. Little is known of any similar incidents that may have occurred earlier in history, but the events that have been documented are worthy of speculation. It is interesting to note the situations, locations, time of year, time of day and so on to find patterns or clues as to why these incidents occurred, thereby giving greater insight into the risks in the event that you do enter polar bear territory. Part of the reason that polar bear attacks are so rare is that the densities of both people and polar bears in the Arctic are low. Also part of it is that most encountered bears are deterred or shot before a human gets harmed. Throughout most of the Arctic, most bear encounters involve people who are well armed, typically Inuit hunters. If a bear cannot be deterred, it is likely to be shot and tallied as part of the annual harvest.

If you do encounter a polar bear and know how to react, the chance of it attacking is very low. Not seeing a bear in time is more dangerous if it is stalking you as prey, but this situation is very rare. Subadult males will often be curious and investigate you, but the use of strong deterrents may cause them to flee. An example from Resolute Bay, Nunavut, shows that during 2003, 146 bear-human interactions (including some multiple incidents with the same bear) were reported between September and November. Four bears that could not be deterred were killed, but the other 142 incidents resulted in the bears being successfully deterred by people shouting, throwing objects at the bear or using items such as bear bangers, rubber bullets or air horns.

If you have the opportunity to see a wild polar bear, consider yourself fortunate—but only if you are seeing it from a safe vantage point!

BASIC IDENTIFICATION

Height to shoulder: up to 1.6 m (5¼ ft) for a large male; standing on his hind legs, he may approach 3 m (10 ft) to his head

Total length: *male:* 2–3 m (6½–10 ft); f*emale:* 2–2.5 m (6½–8¼ ft)

Tail length: 7–13 cm (3–5 in)

Weight: *male:* typically 300–650 kg (660–1500 lb), reaching adult size at 8–14 years; up to 800 kg (1760 lb); *female:* typically 150–300 kg (330–660 lb), reaching adult size at 5–6 years; weight of a pregnant bear typically increases to 400–500 kg (800–1100 lb) prior to entering the maternity den

Hind paw: 30–33 cm (12–13 in) long; up to 23 cm (9 in) wide

Fore paw: shorter than hind paw; not often seen because the hind paws overprint them to optimize walking in deep snow by stepping the hind paws into the tracks made by the fore paws

Fore paw claws: up to 5 cm (2 in) long

Stride: *walking:* 25–50 cm (10–20 in); *straddle:* to 50 cm (20 in)

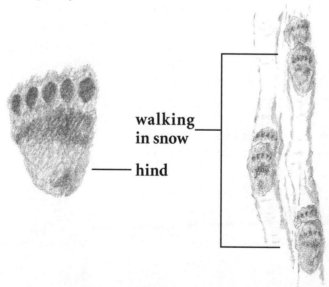

walking in snow

hind

The unmistakable great white bear is the largest bear and largest quadruped carnivore on the planet. Although the polar bear is a terrestrial species, it is an integral part of the marine ecosystem. Because its prey is primarily other marine mammals and because physical adaptations allow this bear to swim for great lengths of time and distance in frigid arctic waters, it is ecologically (and legally in the U.S. but not Canada) recognized as a marine mammal.

The body form is well adapted to swimming as well as preventing heat loss: the body is streamlined, with a small head, small ears, short tail and (typical of most northerly species) short limbs compared to more southerly bear species. The feet are partially webbed, furred between the toes, and the pads have bumps and recesses (papillae) that grip the ice to reduce slipping. Polar bears have been recorded swimming in open water as far as 100 km (60 mi) from shore, at speeds up to 10 km/h (6 mph), and can hold their breath underwater for up to two minutes. They are also capable of climbing difficult icy or rocky terrain and jumping over 2.5 m (8 ft). They are not great runners, rarely running for any length of time or distance because they quickly overheat, but they can reach speeds of 30 km/h (20 mph) in a short burst. They are great walkers, though, and can cover over 160 km (100 mi) in a 24-hour period.

Although the overall colouring of the polar bear appears white to cream, the individual hairs of the fur are actually translucent, and the skin of a polar bear is black. The hollow hairs help insulate the animal from cold, as does the 12-cm (5-in) thick layer of blubber. With its thick undercoat, a polar bear overheats at temperatures above 10° C (50° F). Glossy guard hairs repel water and allow the animal to dry quickly after a swim.

Interestingly, polar bears and grizzly bears are close enough genetically that they can interbreed, and hybrids have occurred in the wild and in captivity. In 2006, the occurrence of this hybrid was confirmed through DNA analysis on a bear shot in the Arctic, where the ranges of the two species overlap. Genetic and fossil evidence now suggests that the polar bear diverged from the brown bear around 200,000 years ago.

WHERE CAN YOU EXPECT TO ENCOUNTER A POLAR BEAR?

Of the world's polar bears (roughly estimated at 21,000–25,000), 60 percent (approximately 15,000) occur in or are shared with Canada's eastern arctic. They are distributed along the coastline of the polar basin and arctic islands on land, landfast ice and permanent offshore pack ice. Within the five "polar bear nations" of Canada, the United States (Alaska), Russia, Denmark (Greenland) and Norway (Svalbard Islands) that comprise the worldwide distribution of the species, researchers have identified 19 distinct polar bear populations. Of these populations, 13 are wholly or partially in Canada, and of those, 12 are at least partially in Nunavut. The Canadian populations range from the northern Yukon in the west to Labrador in the east. On a year-round basis, they are found from within 160 km (100 mi) of the North Pole (88° N) to Ellesmere Island on the permanent pack ice and along all the coastal areas of the Arctic Ocean and Hudson Bay to as far south as James Bay (53° N). On occasion, they are seen farther south, to Newfoundland and the Gulf of St. Lawrence (50° N).

The most well-known and well-studied population of polar bears in the world is in the vicinity of Churchill, Manitoba, where the bears are protected from hunting. They have become part of an active tourism industry wherein tourists are taken in large, bus-like vehicles fitted with enormous tires to safely and readily observe numerous bears a short drive from town. On the western shore of Hudson Bay north of James Bay, Polar Bear Provincial Park is home to 900–1000 bears. At 24,000 ha (59,000 acres), it is Ontario's largest and most northerly park, and it is readily accessible to backcountry adventurers only by air. Few people have had the

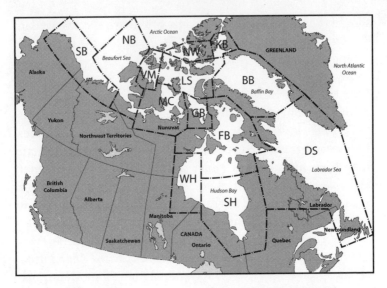

BB - Baffin Bay
DS - Davis Strait
FB - Foxe Basin
GB - Gulf of Boothia
KB - Kane Basin
LS - Lancaster Sound
MC - McClintock Channel

NB - Northern Beaufort Sea
NW- Norwegian Bay
SB - Southern Beaufort Sea
SH - Southern Hudson Bay
VM - Viscount Melville
WH- Western Hudson Bay

opportunity to camp in this remote park, which typically sees only 12–20 visitors per year. Anybody camping along the coast is almost certain to have bears in camp, yet there is no record of a polar bear ever attacking a human in this park.

Studies suggest that five of Canada's 13 polar bear populations seem to be in decline. At least one—the Baffin Bay population—is the victim of severe overhunting, which occurs on the Greenland side of the polar bear's range. Of the three populations that are increasing, the Viscount Melville and McClintock Channel populations (both severely reduced from historic levels) are on the rebound because of the Canadian Inuit's decision to cut back significantly on their harvest. The Gulf of Boothia population is the other population that is increasing, and the Davis Strait population has increased in recent years, but the current trend is unknown.

Dr. Ian Stirling recently reported that his research team has documented a 22-percent decline in the Western Hudson Bay population between 1987 and 2004, further noting that the animals now observed are younger and thinner than was typical 20–30 years ago. The Ministry of Natural Resources in Ontario has reported a similar observation in the Southern Hudson Bay population. With ice melting 2–3 weeks sooner in spring, the animals in these areas are spending more time on land and getting less opportunity to put on the reserves they need to successfully reproduce and to make it through the year. By spring, females with new cubs are on their last fat reserves after a winter of denning and fasting, and their ability to find prey is critical to their lives and their cubs' lives. An early spring melt shortens their already limited hunting season that is necessary to fatten them up prior to the next period of summer fasting.

Most of the southeastern populations go on land in summer and then return to the ice in winter, occurring in "open water" or on "seasonal" ice. The Foxe Basin, Baffin Bay, Davis Strait, Southern Hudson Bay and Western Hudson Bay populations all have open water seasons and seek land retreats until freeze-up. In more northerly areas with multi-year ice, the bears stay on the floating pack ice year-round, but if large areas are ice-free or have only intermittent ice at sea-ice minimums, the bears can be onshore at those times. The bears favour hunting grounds on the sea ice but become more nomadic, venturing inland up to 150 km (100 mi) when the sea ice breaks up or melts.

The loss of ice in summer inhibits the ability to hunt and reduces access to preferred prey, so the bears move off the melting ice and come inland. When the bears come off the ice, they are typically fat from a successful season of hunting and feeding on seals. Once on land, they may stay along the coast or venture inland. Adult males are not aggressive toward people in spring because they are focused on mating; because they are more intent on finding a mate than finding prey, they often fast during the breeding season.

In late fall, after a summer spent roaming the tundra and rocky coastal shores and, for the most part, fasting, the bears begin congregating near the coastlines, awaiting freeze-up. It is along the coast at this late-fall, pre-freeze-up time that polar bears are most conspicuous and dangerous. Males and females without cubs are found closest to the coast and move out onto the ice first, followed later by females with cubs, which hold back to avoid the males, which frequently kill cubs. Pregnant females stay on land, further from the coast, away from the males, to enter their maternity dens to keep their cubs safe from the males.

As the ice thickens, all polar bears move farther offshore and away from the coastal bays and fiords. Some biologists believe that a greater proportion of young and inexperienced seals live offshore amidst broken ice than on or under the landfast ice of the nearshore, potentially offering the bears greater hunting success. If conditions are severe, the bears enter a period of dormancy, seeking shelter in a den (see When Are Polar Bears in Their Dens?, p. 139).

WHAT DO POLAR BEARS EAT?

The polar bear is the only North American bear that preys primarily upon large mammals. As part of the marine ecosystem, it depends on coastal food sources and eats mostly seals. The composition of the diet does vary between populations, but the ringed seal (*Phoca hispida*) is the main prey species for every population. This bear also eats the bearded seal (*Erignathus barbatus*), occasionally the harp seal (*Pagophilus groenlandicus*) and, in the northern Atlantic, the hooded seal (*Cystophora cristata*). Other marine mammal prey include the walrus (*Odobenus rosmarus*), the beluga whale (*Delphinapterus leucas*) and the narwhal (*Monodon monoceros*), although the latter is consumed only as carrion. In late August and September, when much of the ice has melted, polar bears patrol the coast to scavenge walrus, whale and narwhal carcasses. The polar bear also eats shellfish and crabs when available, and it can dive to catch fish such as Atlantic salmon and Arctic char or catch them in the shallows of rivers, but fish are very uncommon prey.

Polar bears often hunt by night, particularly on nights without a full moon so that they do not create shadows over the breathing holes through the ice when they are hunting seals. As with most animals, they are more active at dusk and dawn than at midday—the seals are more active then because the fish they eat are closer to the surface then. Polar bears hunt along the sea ice edge or directly on the ice where it is thin or cracked, along leads, in polynyas (ice-free areas) or out on the permanent pack ice offshore; they also hunt at the toes of glaciers. Rarely, they have been seen to successfully capture seals in shallow areas of bays.

Polar bears use specific modes of hunting: stalking, digging out or still-hunting.

When stalking, the bear either walks or swims discreetly and slowly toward its prey, most often a seal but sometimes a walrus, that is resting at the water's edge on land or an ice floe. If swimming, the bear takes a bearing toward its prey from up to several hundred metres away and then swims the distance underwater, not surfacing until it launches itself directly from the water onto its unsuspecting prey. Polar bears have been documented preying on belugas and minke whales when they come into the mouths of rivers in midsummer and when they come close to the edges of ice floes or the shoreline (where they can even become stranded at low tide), but these occurrences are rare; whale species typically enter the polar bear's diet as carrion. If stalking on foot, the bear first stands motionless at a distance to strategize its attack. It then begins walking directly toward the prey at a steady and determined gait, with head down, sometimes lowering itself into almost a crawl. A charge with impressive speed is used to cover the last 50 m (165 ft) or less.

When digging out, a polar bear uses its acute sense of smell or recognition of shapes in the ice and snow to find lairs where seals lie under the ice resting or rearing pups. The bear approaches the lair in a stealthy, stalking manner to avoid making any noise through cracking ice or crunching snow. When within pouncing distance, the bear launches itself onto the lair, smashing through the ice and either pinning and trapping the seal inside or blocking its escape route to the water. If the bear is well fed, it may kill more than it needs and eat only the fat layer or a select part of the seal, leaving the remains for other bears or other animals to scavenge. Seal pups eventually reach an age when they are almost 50 percent fat, which is optimal for bears. If a very young pup is caught, one without much fat, the bear may kill it but not necessarily consume it. Then the bear may wait for the parent seal to return so that it can be caught and eaten.

When still-hunting, polar bears simply wait at the breathing holes of seals and grab them when they surface.

Polar bears do not cache their kills but consume their fill immediately, before other bears arrive at the scene. Adult polar bears tend to eat only the blubber layer of seals, leaving the rest of the carcass for scavengers. Subadult polar bears, not yet adept at hunting, rely heavily upon this food source, and arctic foxes are commonly seen following polar bears for these feeding opportunities. Other species such as gulls also scavenge polar bear leftovers. A polar bear must catch at least one seal per week to maintain or increase its body mass.

Male polar bears frequently kill and eat polar bear cubs. Often, the mother bear is killed while defending her young and is also partially consumed. Cubs that lose their mother during their first year have little chance of survival.

Along the southern and eastern coasts within polar bear range, the warm season and open water force the bears to hunt from land or swim out to ice floes or permanent pack

ice. The bears may not have a successful hunt for weeks, even months; during these times, the bears are considered to be in a period of fasting. In some areas, "fasting" bears forage on supplemental food sources. Polar bears are opportunistic omnivores, and, particularly during times of food scarcity, they supplement their diet with various foods, including waterfowl and nesting birds (the thick-billed murre is a common bird prey), rodents and berries (common bearberry, soapberry, blueberry, common cranberry and crowberry). They have also been seen to consume kelp and other sea-weeds, lichens, mosses, sorrel, sedges and grasses, all of which supplement their diet but do not supply much food energy. On land, polar bears prey on caribou—and potentially musk-ox calves—and scavenge the carrion of any marine or terrestrial animal that they discover.

It is unknown how much bears eat during this time of fasting, but it is unlikely that foods obtained in this manner would be enough to sustain reproduction if the open-water season were to be significantly extended as a result of climate change. Already, Hudson Bay bears, for example, persist through a very long ice-free season. The landfast ice melts by July or August, not to re-form until late November, by which time pregnant females must enter maternity dens without hunting again until spring. Therefore, they fast for 6–8 months, subsisting on reserves that must sustain them and their nursing cubs. For bears living north of Hudson Bay, the ice-free season is longer than in previous years, adding to the controversy about the effects of global warming on polar bear behaviour and survival.

The bears of the Hudson Bay and Baffin regions are at highest risk to become habituated to human food sources in summer. When the bears are on land and seals are harder to hunt, they may venture into towns and find garbage, or they may track food smells to human camping, hunting or fishing sites to try to steal a meal. They can come to associate human activity with food sources if they encounter such things as food scraps and garbage left by people at camps or townsites and no immediate risk is perceived. In their curiosity, bears have discovered exotic tastes, such as bacon, cheese and fruit, as well as more industrial flavours, including engine fuel, rubber and even snowmobile seats. With their keen sense of smell, they can be drawn to any novel aroma that we would not associate as a food source or temptation to them. Subadults, which are often less skilled at hunting and thus more desperate for food, are especially likely to take on the risk of exploring a campsite or urban environment. A nutritionally stressed female with cubs may also become habituated to human garbage or food sources.

Hunting camps invite a greater frequency of bear encounters than any other type of situation. Northern communities hunt the same species as the polar bear—seal, walrus, beluga and narwhal—and many polar bear encounters occur at the carcass of a hunt or where meat and blubber is stored. Inuit hunters bring meat and blubber back to hunting camps set up near the coast, where it is cached temporarily. Some is eaten during the hunting season, and the rest is brought home to the settlements. Nearby polar bears can easily pick up the scent of this meat and may come to search out the cache or scavenge on garbage. These bears can be dangerous to the members of the camp and are often killed if they cannot be deterred.

The leftover meat and fat from summer whale hunts is an important source of calories at this lean time. Most Inuit whale hunts take place from shore in August and September, when polar bears are unable to hunt on the ice and are hungry, and when many females are either pregnant or accompanied by dependent cubs while surviving only on reserves of body fat. Once the hunting party has taken its share of meat from a whale carcass, the remains are often scavenged by polar bears.

WHEN ARE POLAR BEARS IN THEIR DENS?

Polar bears do not hibernate but do enter dens at various times of the year for several reasons. Dens can sometimes be discovered through tracks leading into or away from a snowdrift, or you may notice a ventilation hole.

In summer, either sex may excavate a sort of den in a snowbank, permafrost, high-elevation snowfield or glacier to escape heat or insects.

Males dig temporary winter dens into snowdrifts or pushed-up sea ice to create a retreat from the elements. The bears can enter a dormant state, remaining in the shelter for days, a week or even longer, but do not have the long winter slumbers that brown and black bears are noted for.

Long-term denning is primarily an activity of pregnant and nursing females. By November or December, pregnant females enter maternity dens made in snowdrifts along the slopes of coastal hills and valleys or at higher elevations on snowfields and glaciers. Breeding season is in spring (April to May), but the implantation of fertilized ova is delayed until fall. Both males and females reach sexual maturity at 4–5 years, but typically, only females breed at that age; males usually begin mating at 8–10 years of age. By January, the female will have given birth in the den to 1–2 (rarely 3) cubs just

30–36 cm (12–14 in) long and weighing 0.6 kg (1.3 lb); the female and cubs stay in the den nursing until the cubs are developed enough to begin exploring the world above the snow. A female polar bear can remain in the maternity den for up to 8 months, during which time she does not eat or drink. By the time she and her cubs leave the den and begin their nomadic search for food, the female is very thin and must immediately find prey. A female will nurse her cubs for at least 20 months, and they will remain with her for an average of 2.5 years, reportedly 3.5–4.5 years in less productive marine areas.

Denning polar bears may be deep sleepers, but they are easily woken. Accidentally stumbling upon a slumbering bear will surprise and threaten it, potentially provoking an attack. If disturbed, females normally defend their dens against intruders, but they may abandon their dens instead, and early den abandonment can be fatal to cubs unable to fend for themselves.

UNDERSTANDING THE MOTIVATIONS AND DANGERS

Polar bears are large and curious and can be aggressive. Young males tend to be more curious than females, and statistics for the number of polar bears killed as a result of a perceived threat to human safety show most to have been males. Attacks on humans are most frequently associated with young male bears, which are believed to be desperate for food as a result of being unable to defend their seal prey from larger males. The most aggressive bears are females with cubs, although where possible, their preference is to avoid encounters for the safety of their cubs.

Curious Behaviour

You may observe a polar bear standing on its hind legs, moving slowly with frequent stops, sniffing the air or trying to catch your scent by moving downwind from you on approach, moving its head from side to side and holding its head high,

with ears forward or to one side. These actions are believed to indicate curiosity, perhaps smelling or listening to something (you). ***Stand tall and upright and speak in a strong, calm tone loud enough for the bear to hear.*** Once most adult polar bears have identified you as human, they will begin to retreat at a fast pace, frequently looking back over their shoulders. Keep your eyes on the bear as long as you can and remain vigilant in watching for its potential return.

Subadult bears, however, are generally more curious and less cautious. It is subadult bears that are most often responsible for human injury or death.

Habituated bears are extremely dangerous, not necessarily because they are intent on preying upon people, but because they lose their fear of approaching people. A natural curiosity and keen sense of smell can attract them to campsites, drill rigs, garbage dumps and contaminants. These lures put both bears and people at risk of injury and death. If, rather than retreating, a bear continues to approach while its behaviour changes to either **aggressive or predatory** in nature, respond accordingly, as described next.

Aggressive or Defensive Behaviour

When a bear lowers its head below its neck, typically with its ears laid back, it is adopting an aggressive or defensive posture. Heightened aggression is displayed by swinging its lowered head from side to side, turning its body to the side and walking stiff-legged or slowly. The most dangerous level of aggression is demonstrated by the foregoing actions accompanied by a clicking, huffing, panting, growling, jaw-snapping or hissing noise, a stomping of the feet and a direct stare—all warning signals that, if ignored, can lead to an attack.

Most often, a hostile bear comes into close range only after circling to get downwind. If attacking, it usually comes at a fast walk and closes the distance travelling in an arc, so that it is not coming directly at its target until the very end. One shoulder leads, the head is held low with the ears back, and the eyes are intent on the person being attacked. Occasionally, a rush is used to cover the very last part of the approach, but usually it is only bears that are surprised or defending cubs (or themselves) that charge. The first charge may be a bluff, but you don't want to risk finding out if it is or

is not. *While keeping the bear in view, without direct eye contact, attempt to back away toward some form of shelter and begin employing whatever deterrents you have at hand.* Remain alert, because the bear's approach may be swift.

A **female with cubs** is strictly focused on caring for her cubs and is very risk averse, defensive and protective. A female with cubs is a beautiful but dangerous sight. Keep every possible distance from a mother bear—she is not only in hunting mode to feed her young, but she is extremely aggressive toward any perceived threat. She may avoid you in order to protect her cubs from whatever threat you may present, or she may attack in defence of her cubs if you surprise her from too nearby or if you appear to be approaching or threatening her and her cubs in any way.

To date, there has never been a report of a female with cubs attempting to prey on a human. Indications are that any human attacks involving a mother polar bear were likely provoked by some form of harassment to the bear (often unintentional), such as threatening, approaching too close or surprising her. It is rare for a female to encounter people, however, as she will do her best to avoid them.

Predatory Behaviour

If a bear is following you, circling, approaching directly without fear, peering over pressure ridges in the ice or repeatedly advancing, it is likely a predatory situation in which the bear is stalking or hunting you. A skinny, hungry bear is very hard to deter. Predatory behaviour is usually first seen, if it is seen at all, with the bear coming in first at a slow, wary stalk, ending in a full-speed charge from a nearby ambush point, its focus intent upon its victim. There is no preceding bluff charge or warning. The bear bites the victim on the head and neck as it would a seal. The intent is not to maul but to kill, thus the chances of survival are very low.

Predatory cases are very rare, however. Humans are a novel prey, and polar bears are risk averse. Hunters affirm that being diligent in scanning the area around you will provide ample time to see a bear before it becomes a threat and to be ready to defend yourself. *Never play dead if attacked by a predatory bear—fight back with all means available.*

ENCOUNTERS

- if you see a polar bear
  - **stay calm; do not show fear**
  - immediately have deterrents in hand and ready for use (see Deterrents, p. 200)
  - do not approach the bear
  - do not feed or use food to distract a bear in attempt to retreat from it
  - never run away from a polar bear; this behaviour may cause the animal to chase you, perceiving you as prey and arousing the instinct to chase
- if the bear is unaware of you
  - do not announce your presence to a bear that has not seen you and is over 100 m (110 yd) away
  - move away quickly, calmly and quietly, keeping your eye on the bear until it has moved out of your vicinity
  - stay downwind and leave the area while keeping watch to see whether the bear notices you and follows
- if the bear is aware of you from a distance but does not advance
  - do not turn your back
  - maintain eye contact but have your head turned sideways (so as not to challenge the bear)
  - if you perceive a way to move out of the bear's path or to a position of safety
    - do not turn away; move sideways or slightly forward, never backward
  - stand (do not sit or lie down) beside a tent, sled or other large object so as to look as large as possible

- o fire warning shots from a firearm or flares to increase the perceived risk for the bear to approach
- if the bear is aware of you and acting curious
  - o do not run; move calmly sideways out of its path or toward some object of protection
  - o if you are fortunate to be near a vehicle
    - ⊙ get in and drive away
  - o if you do not have a car, building or safe area to retreat to
    - ⊙ move slowly (sideways, not backward) upwind to allow it to identify your scent as human
    - ⊙ make sure the bear has an escape route and is not cornered by you in any way
    - ⊙ talk in low tones to identify yourself as human, but if the bear is not deterred, raise your tone and volume to a more aggressive level

- ⊙ make yourself look as large as possible by standing tall or on higher ground and raising your arms above your head
- o if you are with other people
- ⊙ group together
- o fire warning shots from a rifle
- o throw flares into the bear's path
- if the bear is a female with cubs
- o do not come between them in any way
- o immediately distance yourself, but do not run
- o if the female appears to feel threatened by your proximity
  - ⊙ do everything you can to distance yourself
  - ⊙ use deterrents that impress upon her that you would be more of a threat to her cubs if she pursues you than if she takes her cubs and flees
- o if the female is a significant distance away but deliberately approaching you, she may be stalking you as prey (see below)
- if the bear advances
- o do not run, shout or make sudden movements
- o move slowly sideways out of its path or toward some object that may shield you
- o avoid direct eye contact, but keep the bear in your range of view
- o be prepared to use deterrents
- o use a rifle to fire warning shots at the ground directly in front of the bear
- o throw flares into its path
- o if the bear approaches within 50 m (165 ft)
  - ⊙ prepare to shoot
  - ⊙ decide if you can succeed with a nonfatal shot as a deterrent; know your shooting ability—fatally injuring a bear is a less humane death; also, an injured bear may still attack

- ⊙ aim for the hindquarters with a nonfatal plastic slug to avoid injuring the bear's face or eyes
- ⊙ if shooting with a lethal slug, aim for the front shoulder
- if the bear attacks and you have no time for deterrents or lethal force defence
  - o the typical posture of an attacking bear is to come at you with a leading shoulder, so people with experience in these situations have suggested that a person can sometimes step quickly forward to the side of the leading shoulder and have the bear miss on the first pass
  - o experts suggest you lie on the ground and roll yourself into a tight ball, protecting the front of your body and vital organs; clasp your hands over the back of your neck and protect your face with your elbows
  - o if the charge is a false charge, your passive posture may satisfy the bear enough to back away
  - o if the charge is real but defensive, it should be brief
    - ⊙ hold the posture, protecting yourself, and the bear may stop if you are no longer perceived as a threat
    - ⊙ do not move for a considerable time afterward because it may attack again, even if it has moved some distance away
  - o if the attack persists or becomes predatory (the bear starts to bite and chew at your head and neck)
    - ⊙ fight back with any available weapon, including rocks, sticks, shards of ice, knives, tent poles, walking sticks or bare hands
    - ⊙ try to move yourself to find any form of protection
- after any bear has been deterred, it may return; keep a watch around you for several hours

DWELLERS OF THE FLAT BEDROCK

(*written in collaboration with Downs Matthews, co-founder of Polar Bear International*)

Even in modern times, many Inuit families in small northern communities maintain close relationships with the land and still largely subsist on hunting and fishing for meat and pelts. Inuit from Baker Lake, Rankin Inlet, Arviat and other Hudson Bay hamlets traditionally move into tent camps near the shore to fish for Arctic char and hunt for caribou during the short summer season. They know the best areas to fish and hunt and where to find fresh water and ideal camping areas.

Corbett Inlet is one of these special places where the Amitnak family routinely spent summer fishing. It is a small, remote inlet on the west coast of Hudson Bay between Whale Cove, named for the high densities of beluga whales that congregate there, and Rankin Inlet. This area, the Kivalliq Region of Nunavut, is an area characterized by rough, ice-ragged coastlines and austere, rocky beaches. Indeed, the region was once known by the name of *Qairniq*, and the people who lived here the *Qairnirmiut*, "dwellers of the flat bedrock." In spring, the harsh setting is softened by the thaw, and hardy tundra wildflowers splash colour among the bald rocks; in the warm months of summer, Corbett Inlet is accessible by boat—there are no roads there.

Hattie Amitnak (64) had come to Corbett Inlet to camp and fish with her grandson Eddie (10), her friend Moses Aliyak (66) and his grandson Cyrus (12), and her step-daughter Margaret Amarook (56). They were all from the nearby towns of Rankin Inlet and Baker Lake, and they had chosen a spot along the bay to fish and relax. They had set up camp the night before and were just awakening with the sun in the early hours of July 9, 1999, when they discovered that their boat had become untied and had drifted a short distance away along the shore. Moses and Cyrus decided to head off to retrieve it, and Margaret went inland to fetch a canteen of fresh water from a nearby spring while Hattie and Eddie stayed at camp to start preparing breakfast.

Moses and Cyrus could see the boat along the curl of beach, partially obscured by the angle of beach and the large rocks. The water was calm, and the boat was not drifting fast. They leisurely walked along the beach, breathing in the crisp morning air, imagining the good fishing they were to have that day. As they neared the boat, Moses scanned farther up the beach. For a second, he hoped that what he saw was a late-lingering patch of white snow, but he quickly rejected this possibility and realized that there was a polar bear only a very short distance away. The bear just as quickly took notice of the man and his grandson, stood on its hind legs for a moment to confirm the sighting, fell back down to all fours and stead-fastly began to approach them, head swaggering from side to side. Moses began throwing rocks at the bear and firmly ordered his grandson to go back to camp immediately. Cyrus backed away slowly at first but turned and ran as he saw the great bear approaching his grandfather.

The terrified boy ran toward Hattie and Eddie frantically yelling that there was a polar bear. The two leapt up and ran to find Moses doing his best to fend off the assaults of the large, white bear, which towered over him, slashing its great paws across the man's bleeding head.

The sight of Moses under attack caused adrenaline to surge through their veins, and Hattie and Eddie ran selflessly to Moses' aid. The bear knocked Eddie down with a single blow with its foreleg, smashing the young boy's head to the rocks. Then it turned to focus its attentions on Hattie. No longer under attack himself, Moses gathered the young boy in his arms and began to run him to a small, collapsed wooden shack nearby, hoping to return soon enough to help Hattie.

Within a few steps, though, he heard a heartbreaking and shuttering silence slam down upon the scene—her defiant yelling at the bear had stopped. Moses spun on his heels and saw the bear now standing on all fours above the woman. He knew Hattie was dead. Knowing that the bear could quickly turn its sights back on him and Eddie, he continued as quickly and quietly as he could with the unconscious boy, making his way to the small shack while keeping a watch over his shoulder. Blood flowed down his severely mauled face as he looked down at Eddie, and through the panic and shock, Moses had a numb sense of gratitude for the child still alive in his arms, innocent of witnessing the violent death of his grandmother.

Far enough away not to have heard the screaming, Margaret was just returning to camp with a growing eerie feeling in her as she sensed that something was not right. It was unusual that nobody had come halfway up the trail to meet her and help her with the heavy water canteen. With her head down under the weight of the canteen, she had remained oblivious to the cause of the bad feeling. As she neared the campsite and raised her head, she first noticed how void of activity it was. She lifted her gaze a degree higher to see farther up the shoreline and dropped the canteen in shock. She saw the bear and quickly realized that it was standing over a human body; the animal turned its gaze to her only briefly as she ran toward the camp yelling out for her family and friends. She heard Moses return her call and then the voice of Cyrus from the tent warning her of the bear and not to come near. Then as Moses yelled at her to go for help, Margaret saw his bleeding head peer out from the nearby shack.

Although her instinct was to run to help them, Margaret knew that their survival depended upon her getting help. With the bear lingering, she knew the others were still in danger, and help was needed fast. She began to run, glancing back over her shoulder to see Moses leaving the shack with Eddie and moving toward the tent and Cyrus. She ran 3 km (2 mi) to where she knew other friends had a camp with a single-sideband radio to call for emergency aid.

Arriving breathless and still frantic at the camp of David and Rosie Oolooyuk, she wasted no time explaining details, gasping only a rambling of words: "polar bear, two miles down the coast, radio for help!"

David and Rosie, although stunned, leapt into action. David radioed for help while Rosie wrapped a blanket around Margaret and made her breathe and drink some water.

Two helicopters arrived at the camp with RCMP officers and trauma nurses. The bear was no longer at the tragic scene. The campers were evacuated. Moses and Eddie were taken to a hospital in Winnipeg, Manitoba, where they eventually recovered from their injuries.

The RCMP meanwhile called in Gerald Fillatre, a Wildlife and Fisheries officer with the Department of Sustainable Development for Nunavut who had an office in Baker Lake, to deal with the polar bear. After a half-hour search, Gerald found the bear a few kilometres from the campsite and shot it. After inspection, he concluded that the bear had been hunting and had approached the Inuit campsite after smelling its inhabitants.

Death by polar bear is so rare that Inuit communities along the western shore of Hudson Bay were shocked to learn of Hattie's death. According to Gerald, the polar bear-related fatality was the first to occur there in nearly 25 years. "Her behaviour was correct," said Gerald, referring to Hattie's attempt to deter the bear. "Polar bears don't like confrontation and will almost always retreat when challenged," he explained. "But in this case, the bear attacked."

"Destroying the bear was necessary," he went on to say. "Once a juvenile bear has killed a human, it will consider humans a prey species for the rest of its life. Not killing the bear could have put others at risk. Also, we needed an autopsy to determine the bear's physical condition."

Performed in Saskatoon, the necropsy revealed that the bear was less than 2 years old, weighed approximately 115 kg (250 lb), was 1.8 m (6 ft) in length and, although not diseased, was nutritionally stressed and in poor shape.

Dr. Ian Stirling, internationally known polar bear zoologist and bear expert with the Canadian Wildlife Service in Edmonton and author of several books and papers on polar bears, said that, depending on the year, up to 40 percent of adult female polar bears in the southern Hudson Bay population wean their cubs at 1.5 years of age, after which they are free to mate again. Thus, unlike in most other areas of the Arctic, it is not unusual for a bear less than 2.5 years of age in western Hudson Bay to be independent.

"Once on their own," Stirling said, "young bears can have a difficult time for a while because they lack experience in hunting and, even when successful, may have their kills taken away by larger animals. As a result, some animals become hungry, even to the point of starvation, at which time they may be prepared to prey on a human that they would likely otherwise avoid. The autopsy of the bear that killed this unfortunate woman indicated that while the bear was not yet starving, it was in poor condition."

"They were doing everything right," Gerald Fillatre said. "They had a clean camp. Their only mistake was in not having a gun in camp. With a gun, they could have driven the bear away or killed it if necessary."

Polar bears are part of life in the Far North. Inuit residents of Baker Lake embrace a calm, perhaps fatalistic, philosophy about them. Some people wondered if someone had been guilty of thinking bad thoughts about polar bears. "Our elders say that bears can hear a person's thoughts," a Baker Lake native said after the event. "They warn us not to think ill of the bears, for that might make them angry."

Governor General Adrienne Clarkson awarded Moses Aliyak the Medal of Bravery in 2000 for his valiant efforts. Moses continues to live in Rankin Inlet, where he still goes on camping and fishing trips every year.

Hattie Kablutsiak Amitnak's body was returned to her family in Baker Lake. Hattie was awarded the Medal of Bravery posthumously.

POLAR BEAR CAPITAL OF THE WORLD

Churchill, Manitoba, was bestowed with the accolade "Polar Bear Capital of the World" back in 1717 in recognition of the high density of polar bears that inhabit the western coast of Hudson Bay and frequently enter the town in fall. Polar bears had long had high populations in this part of Canada, and a large maternal denning area near present-day Churchill was long well known by native hunters and trappers living in the area. English traders with the Hudson's Bay Company (HBC) first began trading with the natives in this area in 1669, and polar bear hides were a popular trading item. By 1682, the HBC had established a trading post at the mouth of the Hayes River, about 240 km (150 mi) southeast of modern Churchill, and named it York Factory. In 1717, the company built the first of a series of forts and posts in the vicinity of today's Churchill, calling it the Churchill River Post (later Prince of Wales Fort).

It wasn't until 1930 that an act was passed to protect the dens of polar bears and all other fur-bearing animals in the province; however, the hunting rights of First Nations and Inuit were maintained, and trading continued. In 1942, during World War II, an air base (Fort Churchill) was built 13 km (8 mi) east of the town of Churchill, and the men stationed there hunted the beautiful white bear for both its fur and trophy heads to ship home. During this period, any polar bear that came to close to Churchill was shot dead—the meat was fed to the sled dogs, but the beautiful, thick fur was coveted by the townspeople for protection from the cold northern winters. Then, in 1954, additional laws were passed making it illegal for "whites" to hunt polar bears or for anyone to trade or barter in polar bear hides, and by 1957, York Factory closed. In 1964, the Canadian Armed Forces withdrew from Churchill, and by 1965, the base was used primarily by National Research Council (NRC) staff and government personnel. The town became a medical, educational and administrative centre for local Cree and for local Keewatin Inuit.

In the 1960s, the number of bears seen in and around the town began to be noticeably higher—whether the population actually increased or the bears simply became less shy, the lack of hunting seems an obvious factor. With the reduced threat from hunting and the very attractive odours emanating from the town dump, the polar bears were almost taking up residence in town.

The town now had a problem with habituated bears congregating at the local dump to forage for scraps of food or anything else they found palatable. It is remarkable that the townspeople didn't have more frequent incidents, but, all told, only two human deaths attributed to polar bears have occurred in Churchill in the past 50 years. The details of these two incidents differ between sources and are largely recorded in oral history, but they have been pieced together here as best as possible. The first death was in 1968, over 250 years after the town was given its honorary title. At that time, the Churchill area had a population of about 2500, a mixed community of Inuit, First Nations and "white" southerners.

The event took place on a Sunday in mid-November. S.H. Uhrich, an official of the NRC base at Fort Churchill, later stated that there were an unusually large number of bears around Fort Churchill that particular year because of a late freeze-up that had kept them off Hudson Bay. A week before, three polar bears had been shot and killed at the Churchill garbage dump in the hopes that other bears would be deterred by this action. But that would not prove to be the case, and this particular Sunday, the situation seems to have been quite out of control. "They keep congregating in town and at the dump," Uhrich stated. "I saw a dozen at noon Sunday at the dump. They kept walking between the cars, there were about 30 people out taking pictures. And the RCMP were out all day chasing them out of camp."

One bear being chased away took a panicked detour as it made its escape, scattering a group of children returning home from Sunday school. More townspeople got involved in the day's bear-chasing activities, including 19-year-old Paulosie Meeko and his two friends, Billy Tooktoo and David Mickiook, both 16, chasing off the bears by hurling rocks at them. The bears were chased from the edge of the town and watched for a while as they retreated out of sight into the distance. Paulosie and his friends had chased off one bear but had lost sight of him in a nearby area of stunted spruce trees, undulating rock and snowdrifts. Paulosie continued to follow the tracks, intending to continue deterring the bear, just to make sure it had truly left the area.

Losing sight of the bear should have been the first danger signal, and continuing to follow blindly was a grave error. Regardless, following the tracks, Paulosie climbed atop a large drift only to have the agitated bear rear up from below the drift and assault him. Billy and David raced to catch up to their friend and fend of the marauding bear, yelling and hurling rocks at it, but they were not able to make it retreat in time. The bear slashed Paulosie's throat just before it left. The youth was rushed to emergency at the local hospital but died less than two hours after the attack. Uhrich said the bear was shot by police within 20 minutes of the incident.

Fifteen years later, another Churchill man was killed by a polar bear. The details surrounding the incident are vague and seem to be ambling down the path of urban legend. In aptly mysterious fashion, we must push through a smokescreen of time to the scene of a fire. The story is set among the still-smouldering rubble of the incinerated Churchill Hotel, which had burnt to the ground just days earlier.

The flames had been quenched, nobody had been hurt, and the townsfolk had left the cinders to cool. The hotel had a restaurant with a large freezer, which seemed to have been well enough insulated to have survived the blaze with a store of steaks, hamburgers, fish and other perishables intact within. One night, a local man decided to salvage some of this food. As he was loading the meat into the pockets of his parka, a polar bear with a similar interest in the abandoned meat arrived on the scene.

Churchill was still having problems with the habituated bears at the dump; the bears were frequently seen passing through the streets of town, and the locals had learned to be bear-aware, especially at night. This bear had been attracted to the burnt-down hotel. Maybe it was the similarity of the scene to the dump where garbage was burnt in the open, or it could have been the odours of what had burnt in the fire; perhaps the animal could smell the defrosting meat, or maybe it heard the man rummaging, came to investigate and then picked up the scent of the meat. Regardless of the reason, the bear encountered the man at this food source.

The uproar from the attack alerted other people in town, and help quickly arrived on the scene. The bear had by this time killed the man and was dragging him down the street. A local woman tried beating the bear with a broom, but the bear dropped his victim only long enough to charge at the woman and make her back off before returning to his prey. A local wildlife researcher who happened to be in town at the time then ran into the street and shot the bear dead. The bear was identified as a subadult male, likely habituated to the garbage situation of the town, but otherwise healthy.

Today, the residents of Churchill are proud of "their" bears and have learned how to live near them without incident. They have also found the best ways to deter bears from the town, for the bears' safety as well as their own. In 1982, the town established a "polar bear jail," where problem bears can be temporarily detained until freeze-up, when they are released away from town to go off and hunt. More importantly, the troublesome dump was closed in late 2005.

According to Manitoba Conservation, the dump accounted for approximately 60 percent of the bears handled by the relocation program. Garbage is now stockpiled within a secure facility—an old military structure known as Building L5—and later burned, and some recyclables are transported to Thompson, Manitoba. Now that Churchill's trash is properly managed and no longer accessible to the bears, bears are no longer becoming food-conditioned to garbage, and the need for bear relocation has been greatly diminished. Stories still abound, though, of bears walking into soup kitchens, the Legion hall and backyards after following their keen sense of smell to an easy meal, but they are easily scared off by the residents who fearlessly scold them and chase them off with whatever kitchen utensil is closest at hand.

It is estimated that between July and November, 300 polar bears pass by or through the town of Churchill, which lies directly along a migratory pathway for the bears. The small hamlet has become a tourist destination for people to experience the rare privilege of seeing and photographing these animals in the wild. Since 1974, wildlife paparazzi have been coming from all over the world to take the Tundra Buggies out to Gordon Point on the west-central shore of Hudson Bay, approximately 35 km (22 mi) east of Churchill, for close-up views from the safety of the monster-truck–sized vehicles. People ogle at the numerous bears from open windows well above the heads of the bears, although, when standing on their hind legs, some of the larger bears can reach the tips of their black noses to the windows.

On at least one occasion, a photographer reached his arm out of the window to better angle his camera at a bear he was shooting, not noticing another bear under the window that then proceeded to grab his arm and inflict some damage. Overall, the bear watching is remarkably incident free, though, and the bears seem quite used to human presence... which raises some concerns about this situation being yet another form of habituation.

POLAR BEAR MAN

A true northerner, Kootoo Shaw is of Inuit heritage and knows well the polar wilderness of Nunavut where he was born and raised. Now in his 40s, he has worked for many years as a guide for the Hunters and Trappers Association. When not working, he loves to trek out onto the snow with his two dogs, Goofy and Cleo, a couple of small but mighty mongrels capable of pulling a *kamotiq* (Inuit sled) loaded with a sleeping bag, Coleman stove, rifle, seal meat and bannock. At night, Kootoo builds himself a small igloo in which to sleep. By day, he is entertained by sightings of wolf, fox, ptarmigan, rabbit, caribou and, rarely, polar bear. On the night of September 1, 2003, he got closer to one than desired.

Kootoo had been hired by a group of three American caribou hunters from Wisconsin. At the time of the encounter, they were three days into their expedition. They had set up camp near the small Inuit community of Kimmirut and had long been asleep in their tents, slumbering in the arctic silence. They did not hear the young bear stealthily enter their camp at 4 AM, perhaps drawn in by the scent of the caribou carcasses from their successful hunt. It was only when the bear tore through the Americans' tent that the occupants awoke in terror, soon realizing that they had left their guns well out of reach, in the boat. Their screams and shouts deterred the marauding bear only so far as to divert its attentions to the second tent, from which Kootoo was just emerging.

It has been suggested that several errors in judgement and a misunderstanding of the firearms laws were responsible for the terrifying situation in which the hunting party now found itself. Supposedly, the men had been motivated to unload and remotely store their firearms because they were going to be drinking and wanted to avoid an accident, and, although it is true that alcohol does not mix well with firearms, it also definitely does not mix well with bears. In addition, the guide and hunters had apparently misinterpreted the laws on firearms, claiming that they understood that ammunition had to be removed when the gun was idle and that guides were not allowed to carry loaded firearms while guiding foreigners, so Kootoo did not have a rifle at hand either.

In all the excitement, the bear—a young, inexperienced subadult male—pounced on the unarmed guide. The bear knocked Kootoo flat on his stomach and continued to pound its weight onto the unfortunate man by jumping its upper body up and down. Reacting by instinct, the young bear was treating this frantic mammal beneath him as prey, using the same technique that bears use to break through the thick ice to catch seals in their ice chamber dens. The impact broke several of Kootoo's ribs. The bear then proceeded to tear at its prey, scratching Kootoo across the body and biting and ripping at his scalp. The attack was so fast that Kootoo was still conscious and aware of every assault as well as the bear's panting breath. Kootoo held his hands over the back of his neck, knowing that if the bear latched its jaws around his neck, it would be the final, lethal technique—his neck would be snapped.

Then a shot rang out, and the bear fell dead at Kootoo's side. While the guide was being attacked, one of the hunters had run to the boat, retrieved a gun and delivered a clean, lethal shot that saved Kootoo's life.

Although he was still alive, Kootoo had multiple bites and slashes on his back, arms and feet, broken ribs and a lifted scalp. The men drove Kootoo to the town of Kimmirut by ATV as quickly as they could, given that they were unable to rush over the uneven terrain, where every bump was agony. For two hours, the men kept Kootoo from going into shock. When they arrived at the Kimmirut Health Centre, the Inuit guide was med-evacuated to Baffin Regional Hospital in the Nunavut capital of Iqaluit. There, he received more than 300 staples to reattach his scalp, 20 stitches in his back and treatment for two broken ribs and his other injuries.

Experts assess this incident as a fairly classic polar bear attack, with the bear sneaking in just before dawn and making a predatory assault. The attack occurred in September, when the bears are hungriest, awaiting freeze-up. The bear was a young male, likely 3–5 years old, big enough to be dangerous but small enough to have a tough time competing for food with larger bears. It was exploring its options. Tragically, if the men had had their guns at hand, they may have been able to deter the young bear by shooting into the air to startle it away, perhaps continuing to shoot at the ground in front of the bear if necessary. At the very least, had the bear not been deterred, they could have shot it before it attacked anyone.

It is unclear whether the caribou meat was cached at a distance from the camp or not, and whether or not the men had been cooking at their camp; nonetheless, a bear could have been in the area by chance or even have found the cache at a distance and then gone on to explore other opportunities in an otherwise clean and properly established camp. Risk is inherent when camping in the Arctic.

"I thought I was going to die," Kootoo told reporters at the time. "It was the scariest thing that has ever happened to me." Yet, he is not deterred from returning to the wilderness he loves. He acknowledges the potential danger but appreciates that this risk affirms the wildness of the land. Nine months after his recovery, Kootoo embarked upon a five-day trek from Kimmirut to Iqaluit to raise money for hockey equipment and an arena for kids in his community. "We've been trying to get that arena for 15 years, and we've been turned down," Kootoo said. Constructing an arena for the small South Baffin hamlet of 400 residents, he explained, would give local youth a greater quality of life and the community a place for recreational activities and events.

Since then, the tiny town of Kimmirut did get its arena, and Kootoo Shaw has continued to give talks to local schools about wildlife, including polar bears and his experience—for a while, he became a local celebrity, with wide-eyed kids calling him the "Polar Bear Man."

EXPECT THE UNEXPECTED

An attack similar to the one that befell Kootoo Shaw occurred a few years earlier on Soper Lake, about 15 km (9 mi) from the small Inuit town of Kimmirut. Another dawn attack, it happened in the early morning of July 27, 2001. Four Québécois campers—Éric Fortier (orthodontist, 32), Anne Dumouchel (dentist, 33), Alain Parenteau (pharmacist, 31) and Patricia Doyon (speech therapist, 25)—were on a week-long canoe trip down the Soper River, which flows through Katannilik Territorial Park. This story takes place on the last day of their trip. All but Patricia had extensive outdoor experience. Éric and Anne had made annual backcountry hiking sojourns throughout Canada, but this was their first arctic adventure.

It had been a relaxing river journey, with only basic white-water, and the foursome was anticipating a last leisurely paddle across Soper Lake to the take-out, which was only a few kilometres by road from Kimmirut. They had spent the week watching caribou graze along the riverbanks and fishing for Arctic char in the oxygen-rich waters fed by rainwater and snowmelt. Tumultuous waterfalls cascade from the high valley walls—the area's Inuit name, *Katannilik,* means "land of falling water." The weather had been lovely, with little rain, comfortable temperatures and only gentle winds and lolling waters pushing their canoes down the meandering river.

At the start of their trip they had met with park officials to report their itinerary, but they had not seen another person since they pushed off, and it now felt as if they had the park to themselves. They had been unmolested by bugs or bears. Even sighting a polar bear on the popular Soper route would be a rare event because it is inland, and polar bears stay mainly on the coast; several guides confirmed that they had never seen a polar bear on this stretch of river in the numerous decades they had been guiding. Indeed, this lack of bears was one of the reasons the two couples had chosen the Soper. However, their trip was about to undergo an abrupt change of pace.

Camped along Mount Fleming within a lush tundra valley that broadens as it reaches 60 km (40 mi) toward the sea, the group had unknowingly pitched their tents directly in the path of a young polar bear making its way down the valley toward the coast.

The history of this particular bear that took it up the valley in the first place would later come to light. Earlier that summer, the bear had been near the town of Kimmirut and had become somewhat conditioned to discoveries of human garbage, and on more than one occasion it had approached local people camping by the coast. None of these encounters had resulted in any injuries because the local people were able to deter the bear from their camps. But there were a few too many close calls, and eventually, officials were called upon to deal with this "nuisance bear." It was driven out of the Kimmirut townsite with force, by shooting near it, chasing it with skidoos and bear bangers and plugging it with rubber bullets for several kilometres—up the Soper Valley.

The polar bear was first sighted by a larger party of tourists that had reached the lakeshore the day before the two Québécois couples arrived on the scene. The guide took the time to report the sighting to another guide she knew in the area because it was unusual (although not impossible) for a polar bear to be in this location, so far inland in the mountainous highlands of southern Baffin Island. Both guides and their groups camped together, and their final night on the river passed with no consequence, perhaps because the large size of their camp, with numerous tents, was too much of a risk for the young bear to explore. The next day, the bear was reported to park officials, and a warden came to investigate. He was unable to find anything but tracks; the bear appeared to have left the area. Not knowing that a bear had been seen in the area the previous day, the four canoeists set up their final camp of the trip.

In the twilight hour of 3 AM, the bear reappeared. It encountered the small campsite, with its two strange, flimsy domes. It sniffed at the first one and pushed against it. The odd dome was not firm like ice, the bear discovered, but could be pushed in—and now it was pushing back! We might wonder if the bear thought to itself that there might be a tasty seal inside this strange snowdrift, but that is sheer speculation. The bear swiped at the tent, found potential prey inside and reacted. Perhaps frightened by the screaming and yelling of Éric and Anne inside, the bear moved away, only to attack the next tent, where Patricia and Alain were now awake and attempting to get out the side door.

Even on all fours, the bear was nearly as tall as Alain—the campers estimated him to be standing 1.5 m (5 ft) from head to ground—and it easily pounced upon him, pushing him to the ground. In nightmarish horror, the bear clawed repeatedly at Alain's head as he lay on his back trying to shield himself with his arms, which as a result were being slashed. Kicking at the bear as he tried to wriggle away resulted in a bite to his left thigh as well. All the while, his three friends were yelling and hurling rocks at the marauding animal. The bear then turned on Patricia, threw her onto the ground and began slashing her head, back and thigh. Anne screamed at Patricia to roll into a ball.

Éric then leapt at the bear with his 10-cm (4-in) pocket knife and began stabbing it in the neck. The knife was too short to penetrate deeply, but it drew blood and seemed to discourage the bear from further attack upon this difficult and tenacious prey. The bear merely lurched away from his assailant with the knife, abandoned his intentions with Patricia and lumbered dejectedly down to the shore, thankfully in the opposite direction from the canoes toward which the four panicked friends made a mad dash. Quickly grabbing their gear, they threw it and themselves into the canoes and pushed off in the direction of the town of Kimmirut.

The attack had lasted mere minutes, but time had lost significance in the panic. Now, the hours of paddling to safety seemed to drag even more painfully long. Patricia and Alain had sustained severe injuries and were too weak to paddle. Éric and Anne lashed the canoes alongside each other, wrapped their friends in sleeping bags and leaned into their paddles with all their strength. Alain was already shivering. Éric and Anne kept talking to the other couple, hoping they would not go into shock. They kept their eyes on the shore, anxiously watching for the bear. A polar bear would not be deterred by the water, and the canoes were not any safer than being on land. The bear could easily capsize the small craft, and bears are far more agile in water than humans. The cold water would further imperil their chances of survival.

But their fears proved needless: the bear was not to be seen again, and the town soon came into view. It was still early, around six in the morning, when they reached their take-out point at Kimmirut. Several hours had passed since the attack, and it was only now that Alain said that he began to feel the pain. Éric left Anne to care for the victims as he ran the few kilometres into town for help and returned by RCMP truck with the local nurse, who treated the victims until the medevac flight arrived soon after to evacuate them to the Baffin Regional Hospital in Iqaluit. Alain was in surgery by the afternoon. He had severe wounds to his scalp, with nerve damage, but he and Patricia would be fine. The four friends were soon reunited and undeterred from planning their next camping trip. Their experience of survival had only made them more appreciative of living life to the fullest and loving nature despite its inherent dangers.

The following year, Éric was presented with the Medal of Bravery at Ottawa's Rideau Hall by Governor General Adrienne Clarkson.

Immediately following the attack, Katannilik Territorial Park was closed while wildlife officers searched for the bear, but it was never found. The park was reopened within a few days, but, since this nearly tragic event, park authorities make a point to remind visitors to be wary of polar bears, despite their rarity in the area.

ARCTIC EXPLORERS AND ADVENTURERS

To illustrate just how rare polar bear attacks causing human death really are, we have to look back to the journals of historical arctic explorers. Although the accuracy of such ancient and heroic tales remains disputable, they serve to show just how far back in the human psyche dwells the fear of the great bear. In "The Polar Bear" in *The Mariner's Chronicle*, we are told what transpired on the 1596 voyage for the discovery of the Northeast Passage when Dutch explorers Barentsz and van Heemskerk anchored their ship at an island near Waygatz Strait. The book recounts how two men walked ashore, and one was seized from behind—by a polar bear. The second man, seeing his crewmate in the embrace of the bear, ran back to the ship screaming, "a bear!" When he returned to the scene with reinforcements bearing pikes and muskets, the bear left its first victim and grabbed a second. The crew fled back to the ship, mustered up their strength and returned again to kill the bear.

The demise of most other mariners on these northern exploratory expeditions was attributed to exposure or starvation rather than polar bears. Such was the fate as told by the Inuit of Pelly Bay of the infamous and disastrous 1845 Franklin expedition to discover the elusive Northwest Passage. The graves of three men are marked, and they are a sombre component of most interpretive tours to visit the area.

Unlike the early Europeans, the Inuit have a much more brotherly portrayal—rather than a monstrous one—of the polar bear. They believed that the polar bear would approach a man only with the desire to be killed so that it would go into the afterlife as a human. When the bear was killed, the hunter would honour the kill and offer it food and weapons for the afterlife in exchange for its fur. Freed of its fur, the kindred bear would acknowledge the good acts of the hunter, and in return, no polar bear would kill the hunter. Believing that each polar bear is a man trapped in bear's clothing, this exchange is considered a fair negotiation.

One of the first "whites" to live within the northern communities, as chronicled in several of his books, in particular *My Life With the Eskimo,* was famous arctic explorer Vilhjálmur Stefánsson—after whom Stefansson Island, at the tip of Victoria Island, is named. He had learned how to avoid a fatal encounter with a polar bear and speaks of only one occasion where he had to shoot a bear that had stalked him to within a few metres before Stefánsson took notice and had to exercise very quick reflexes to avoid the potential attack.

Europeans and their descendants continued to explore the Arctic in races of glory to be the first to discover new passages, the first to arrive at the North Pole, the first to visit the Magnetic North Pole, the first to arrive by dogsled, the first to arrive by foot, the first to arrive alone. Although the native people of the Arctic were already familiar with every frozen nook and cranny of their homeland, had surely traipsed enormous distances in their nomadic lifestyles and were the best adapted and most knowledgeable to meet these challenges, they humbly, and ironically, left these glories for the pursuit of a different culture of men.

And then the women got into the game. The first white woman to trek solo to the Magnetic North Pole was Helen Thayer, inspiring womenkind as well as gaining recognition among the leagues of fellow explorers. She started her adventure in March 1988 from Resolute Bay in Nunavut (Northwest Territories at the time). Whereas her southern supporters cheered her on, the Inuit raised concerns about her limited understanding of polar bears. They gave her a crash course in arctic survival, and Helen spent two weeks studying under their tutelage. Finally, they relented to say that it was fine by them if she wanted to go without other people, but she would not survive alone. Therefore, they insisted that she have a dog accompany her. Although he was a mongrel, Charlie was a skilled arctic explorer in his own right and had proven his muster to his owner, an Inuit polar bear hunter. Charlie would prove more valuable than any other companion to Helen on her "solo" trek.

Helen would soon come to heed the Inuit's sage warnings when her new knowledge and Charlie's bear-chasing skills were put to the test. In her book, *Polar Dream*, she tells of two harrowing encounters of the polar bear kind in just a single day. One encounter was with a female bear with two cubs. Charlie saw the bears first and alerted Helen by his growls. The woman was just packing up her tent to start the day's trek when she heard the dog's long, low growl. She could have guessed at what was agitating him but looked up without a split second's hesitation and followed his stare to see the bears at a distance of only about 200 m (220 yd). The female was moving toward Helen and Charlie with a deliberate gait, and the two cubs were loping behind. Helen's adrenaline began rushing and Charlie began barking. Helen made a warning shot with her .338 and then began shooting hot flares in front of the mother bear's approaching steps. As each flare landed in the bear's path, she stopped and veered around it, only to have another flare land in front of her.

There were only about 100 m (110 yd) separating them, and Helen had shot six flares, before the bear finally stopped and focused on the savage barking and growling coming from Charlie. She looked back at her two cubs, then seemed to abandon any notion that these two strange animals would be suitable prey. This mama bear appeared quite willing to steer her young ones away from the crazed aggression being demonstrated.

The greater danger to this mother bear's cubs, however, was a large male of the species not far away. Helen encountered this second threat all too soon, just one hour after her first fright. She tells of her shock and anguish at barely recovering her nerves from the first encounter before spotting the next bear 400 m (440 yd) downwind and moving toward her. Charlie, this time, was silent. Helen followed Charlie's lead and held still, watching the bear. When the bear was a mere 45 m (150 ft) away, she again grabbed her rifle and gave a warning shot followed by a sequence of flares, but the bear was neither distracted nor deterred. She went to release Charlie's clip from the chain that attached him to the sled, and at that moment, the dog leapt into the air and emitted a loud, ferocious, snarling growl that stopped the bear in its tracks. Helen fired more flares, and the bear changed direction and moved off in a wide arc away from them. Charlie went silent again, and he and Helen watched the bear leave. The bear also looked back over its shoulder from time to time, and then it was gone.

What Helen points out to be particularly interesting in retrospect is how differently Charlie reacted during the two encounters. Barking like a mad dog at the mother with cubs—Charlie seemed to inherently know that a mother bear's main concern is to protect her cubs—was the necessary response to deter this first bear. The second bear, however, was either a subadult male or a more elderly adult male. The former is typically curious and unsavvy, whereas hunters and researchers have observed the latter to normally be wary of potential danger. The well-timed assault of barking and flares would have potentially made a subadult too nervous to consider further investigation or given an adult bear the proper warning that the situation had become dangerous.

Keep in mind the time of year as well: late March. The mother bear was likely hunting and soon realized that a seal pup under the ice was a much safer and available prey than an aggressive human and dog. Helen described the male bear as "large and powerful," so it was likely not starving after hunting throughout winter. The foregoing is speculation, but, considering the situation and time of year, it is a plausible assessment.

Helen Thayer's story is a fascinating account by a very courageous woman who stood her ground on these two occasions without firing the fatal bullet—other adventurers may not have been as brave. The time she took to understand the motivations and behaviour of polar bears and how to coexist with them in their territory not only saved her life but also spared the lives of four bears. Helen achieved her goal, and the book in which she shares her experiences and her love of the Arctic is a poignant and inspiring read.

WORKING IN POLAR BEAR COUNTRY

The first series of the following events took place in 1975. It was January, a time of year when the light of the sun begins shyly returning to the horizon at far northern latitudes, contributing only a pale glow to the arctic landscape, initially for perhaps only a fraction of an hour that defines day from night. People living and working in the High Arctic get accustomed to carrying out their activities in an artificial light that cuts through the darkness.

It was on one of these dark mornings that two men were working on an oil-drilling barge in the Canadian Beaufort Sea. The barge was frozen within the grips of the ice that clutched it solidly just north of the mouth of the Mackenzie River. As the story goes, the two men decided that it was time for a warm-up and a coffee break back at the mess hall. One man went ahead, and the other indicated that he would soon follow. The first man made his way back to the hall in the dark and waited. As the minutes passed, he began to wonder what was taking his colleague so much longer. He turned back to where they had been working, but there was no sign of him. The man immediately rounded up the other 70-some crew-members and began a search.

Returning to the area of the barge where the missing man had been working, the search party also found no sign of him. But they did notice scratch marks on the door that had obviously been made by a polar bear. They waited until midday for that brief performance from the timid sun to shed some light upon their mystery. In the eerie glow, they ventured out onto the ice and soon found bold smears of blood on the white snow—and then the man's head. Not far away, they saw the bear as it rose on its hind legs, impressing its 2.4-m (8-ft) height upon the men. Then it dropped back to all fours and grabbed hold of the man's body with its jaws and shook it in a manner much like that of a dog or cat with a chew toy. Nobody had a gun; the men tried shooting a flare gun to scare off the bear but the gun froze up and would not fire.

Desperate to retrieve their colleague's body, some of the men returned to the barge and got a forklift that they then tried to drive toward the bear, but it just kept carrying its prey farther onto the ice. Giving up, they called upon the RCMP, who eventually flew in and shot the bear. When the men were finally able to approach, they saw the bear up close for the first time. It had a metal tag in its ear, which soon provided the information that this bear was only two years old. The winter of 1975 was its first winter hunting on its own.

Two years before, in 1973, a seismic operation in the Beaufort Sea, this time near Kendall Island, had lost one of its crewmembers to a polar bear attack. The victim was a cat operator. He had just finished his lunch in the mess hall and was leaving at the same time as the cook. As he was walking down the staircase that exited the building, preceded by the cook, a polar bear that was hiding behind the building leaped out and struck him with a lethal blow to the back of the head. The man was killed with this single blow; the attack came without warning, and likely the man did not even see the bear approach. The cook escaped unharmed.

Many bear problems occur at industry camps and work sites such as the ones above. These large rigs, camps and crews are extremely conspicuous on the empty sea ice. Polar bears in the area easily pick up the buffet of aromas emanating from people, food, fuel and so on. If hunger or curiosity lures them in too close, human-bear incidents are a certainty, and the results can be tragic if the bear comes in unnoticed.

*   *   *

On July 1, 1961, Tony Overton and three colleagues from the Canadian Department of Energy, Mines and Resources were conducting seismic studies on sea ice near the southwest coast of Ellef Ringnes Island, which is in the far north of what is now Nunavut. They had seen signs of neither bear nor seal during the time they were camped in the area, so, when some water accidentally got spilled inside their tent, they opted to sleep outside rather than in the damp. The weather was mild, and they were on dry ground. They set up their sleeping bags in a row near the tent and placed a rifle close at hand, just in case.

Something in Tony's subconscious instincts roused him from his sleep at 4 AM. He opened his eyes just in time to see a polar bear approaching him from about 65 m (200 ft) away. In a flash, he grabbed for the rifle lying beside him, but the bear was on him in those few seconds. It grabbed him by the arm and dragged him 15 m (50 ft) as he yelled for his colleagues to save him. Bill Tyrlik awoke and grabbed the rifle. The bear immediately dropped Tony and turned to charge Bill. Without time to aim, Bill made a lucky shot from the hip and managed to hit the bear right between the eyes. The bear dropped at the foot of Bill's sleeping bag.

*   *   *

Polar bear researchers for the Government of Nunavut (Department of Environment, Wildlife Research Section) work with polar bears that they tranquilize with darts so they can work on the animals in slumbering safety. However, as long-time researcher Dr. Mitch Taylor recounts, close calls from time to time keep them alert. In one incident that started out as a routine capture and sedation of a mother and two cubs, he was so engrossed in his work on the three that he didn't notice the approach of a subadult male bear. Mitch saw the bear in time to grab his revolver and shoot into the snow before it several times, thus deterring it and giving the other researchers time to return to their helicopter and start it. The noise from the helicopter caused the bear to move off. Once the helicopter was ready to fly, they chased the subadult a good distance away from the female and cubs. They then darted him as well, giving him a slightly higher dose so that he would not awaken before the female and cubs and harm them. Now the researchers had four bears to work on!

Dr. Ian Stirling, the polar bear zoologist who was quoted in an earlier story (see p. 148), states that during his years of research tagging bears, he only once had to defend himself when a tranquilizer dart did not function properly. As the angered bear charged him, he barely had time to grab a rifle and shoot it.

It is when researchers are working in field cabins that they are at the greatest risk of polar bear encounter. Again, most often it is subadult males, with their great curiosity, that are involved—the bear that had attacked Tony Overton in 1961 was also a subadult male. Dr. Lily Peacock, Nunavut's Polar Bear Biologist, tells of numerous occasions where they had individual bears seemingly offer themselves up for study. They approached the cabin so closely that the researchers could easily tranquilize them from the front door.

Almost always, these individuals were found to be subadult males. Sometimes these bears had earlier been observed sleeping or resting on the ice in the distance until dusk when, "like clockwork," Lily explains, they stood up, set their sights on the cabin and walked directly over to investigate.

We can only hope that, on awakening, the subjects of the research consider it to have been a sufficiently negative experience that they do their best to avoid any future encounters with humans.

Avoidance Techniques Against Bear Encounters

AVOIDANCE TECHNIQUES AGAINST BLACK BEARS AND GRIZZLY BEARS

The following lists of safety tips pertain to the various situations in which people have commonly found themselves in bear country. These situations are much more diverse than those in polar bear territory, and most safety procedures are identical for avoiding encounters with both black bears and grizzly (brown) bears. Specific considerations for safety in grizzly bear territory are explained at the end of this section. Polar bears are treated separately.

The most common situations in which people find themselves having to consider the presence of black bears or grizzly bears usually involve outdoor leisure or work activities, such as hiking, biking, camping or picnicking, berry or mushroom picking, fishing or hunting, mending fences or surveying. Often, the settings for these situations are foreign to the people involved, particularly if they are tourists, either from abroad or from elsewhere in Canada—or they may simply have rarely ventured beyond the comforts of the city. Hiking, walking and biking in bear country involve safety considerations that may not be obvious to a person who has only previously done these activities where bears do not exist. When visiting a park, campground or recreational area, be sure to check at the visitor centre or information display to find out if bears are likely to be in the area and what precautions and safeguards are advised.

People who live either seasonally or year-round in bear country have to think long-term about not creating a situation that is likely to attract bears near their home, cabin, work camp, summer camp, farm or ranch. Most people in these settings are familiar with the risks, but some people may be new residents, such as retirees who are moving into cottage country or their retirement home in the country or their new dream home on an acreage. Still other people may be spending a season in bear country for holidays or for work. Canadians find themselves cohabitating with bears in many scenarios; the lists of safety tips attempt to consider the most common of these scenarios. Most provincial and territorial governments are developing bear smart campaigns to reduce economic losses and public danger for their residents and visitors. The following lists include the recommendations laid out by the various Canadian government agencies in addition to the many sources of information on bear safety.

Hiking Safety
- before your hike, leave details of your route and anticipated return time with authorities or friends (and be sure to check in with them on your return)
- carry deterrents (see Deterrents, p. 200)
- where possible, choose routes with good visibility
- avoid hiking at dusk and after dark
- don't hike with earphones or headphones—they could prevent you from hearing a bear
- do not wear perfume or use perfumed cosmetics, soaps or shampoos; avoid bringing cosmetics that emit strong fragrances

- eliminate or reduce odours from food or garbage; do not bring pungent foods (such as meat and fish), choose suitable odour-proof packaging and minimize unnecessary packaging
- do not hike alone; the larger the group, the less likely a bear will approach you or remain in the vicinity
  o stay in a close group, not allowing one person to lag behind or one person to rush ahead
  o keep young children close to you at all times
- stay on the trail
  o if you need to leave the trail, or the trail becomes intermittent, do your best to remain in open areas with good visibility
- stay alert and look ahead for bears; be especially cautious in areas where visibility or hearing is obstructed by dense brush or running water
- avoid hiking along game or bear trails, which can often be identified by height—if you have to crouch or crawl to pass through a tunnel-like passage through vegetation, you are likely on a bear trail
  o if you must pass, do not linger; stay alert and make your presence well known by making noise
- approach thickets from upwind if possible
- make noise—whistle, sing, talk loudly or play a radio—to alert bears of your presence
- keep dogs on leashes and under control at all times—a loose dog may lead a bear back to you
- if you find fresh signs of bear activity, such as tracks, droppings (size reflects the body mass of a bear; typically in a mound or stack, not tubular or in long streaks; likely to contain vegetation, berries or fur—see Additional Avoidance Techniques against Grizzlies, p. 192), diggings, tree rubbing or chewing, leave the area
- watch for bear food sources, such as carcasses, torn-up stumps or rotten logs and berry patches (see What Do

Black Bears Eat?, p. 23, and What Do Grizzly Bears Eat?, p. 76)
- use binoculars to scan the area ahead and around you periodically and when you have open vistas
- if you see a bear, calmly leave the area

Mountain Bike Safety
- before your bike trip or ride, leave details of your route and anticipated return time with authorities or friends (and be sure to check in with them on your return)
- carry deterrents (see Deterrents, p. 200)
- avoid biking at dusk and after dark if possible
  o if you do ride in the dark, use a strong light
- avoid biking alone; riding in groups increases your noise level and your ability to be a larger force to deter an encountered bear, and, if an attack takes place, some cyclists can help the victim while others can go for help
  o if riding with children, keep close to them at all times
- don't ride with earphones or headphones—they could prevent you from hearing a bear
- cycle on established trails and be cautious when approaching blind corners
- avoid sneaking up on a bear, as is easily possible when moving quickly on a bike, either turning tight corners on a trail or moving through bush; the risk of mountain biking in bear country is that you move quickly and quietly, making an accidental surprising of a bear with close encounter more likely; reduce speed and make noise in areas of low visibility or on winding paths with a limited view ahead
- avoid trails in dense, shrubby areas, especially ones lined with berry bushes

- avoid racing at high speeds, especially where visibility alongside or ahead on the trail is limited—if a bear were to appear before you on the trail, you would have a difficult time stopping your approach and would reduce your time to react
- make noise; shout, sing or use loud bike horns or bells to alert bears of your approach
- be cautious if hearing is obstructed by the sound of strong wind or running water
- if you find fresh signs of bear activity or food sources (see Hiking Safety, p. 175), leave the area
- if you spot a bear from a distance, leave the area and find an alternative route
- if you encounter a bear at close range, step off your bike and back away on foot, keeping the bike between you and the bear; do not try to outrun or out-cycle the bear

Hunting Safety

- hunt with a licenced outfitter—in some Canadian jurisdictions, doing so is mandatory
- in addition to your rifle or bow, carry bear spray and know how to use it; even if you manage to shoot a charging bear, it will often live long enough to follow through on its attack upon you and inflict harm
- avoid hunting alone—bears are less likely to attack people in groups
- because hunters must remain quiet when stalking game, the chances of accidentally sneaking up on a bear are greatly increased; be astutely aware of your surroundings, and although you are already keeping your visibility and hearing unobstructed, think about your place in the food chain and in animal hierarchy—you are not the only hunter—a black bear may see you as prey—and, if you unknowingly threaten a bear, you may not have the time or the range to save yourself from attack

- avoid places with flocks of noisy crows or ravens, which are attracted to carrion upon which a bear may also be feeding
- be aware of inadvertently attracting bears when calling game—these sounds may attract bears to what they believe to be an animal in distress
- know how to properly cache your game kills and be particularly cautious when in the process of caching or moving it; have one person on watch for bears while the other handles the carcass
- if you find fresh signs of bear activity or food sources (see Hiking Safety, p. 175), leave the area
- avoid dressing your kill near your campsite, and leave any gut piles well marked and out of the path of other people in the area; inform the authorities of your activities

  Note: Criminal charges are a definite possibility if you shoot a bear without a permit or out of season or if you shoot a female with cubs at any time and cannot prove it was in self-defence (shooting from a long distance or from behind does not prove the bear was a threat); hunting bears is permissible only in certain jurisdictions, in specified seasons, with a permit.

Fishing Safety
- carry deterrents (see Deterrents, p. 200)
- fish with at least one other person, and watch around each other's positions for bears; the larger the group, the less likely a bear will hang around
- avoid fishing along shores lined with thick vegetation (especially berry-bearing shrubs) or sections of river with visibility obscured by sharp bends or steep or rocky shores

- if fishing in noisy running water, be even more aware of visibility up- and downstream and upland from both streambanks; look around frequently
- talk loudly and make a lot of noise along streams
- clean fish at designated fish-cleaning stations if possible
  - if there are none, use a fast-moving section of river far from any campsites downstream and ensure that there are no bears nearby; one person should watch for bears while a second person cleans the fish
- store fish in the water to reduce odour; steel-mesh bags are available to protect the fish from animals if you wish
- store food and remains away from your campsite
- if you find fresh signs of bear activity or food sources (see Hiking Safety, p. 175), leave the area
- if you see a bear, calmly leave the area

Tenting Safety

- explore within at least 100–150 m (110–165 yd) of your proposed camping area for fresh signs of bear activity or food sources (see Hiking Safety, p. 175) before setting up camp; be prepared to choose a new location if you find any
- pitch your tent in an open area; avoid setting up near dense brush or trees, under cliffs or ridges, next to a lakeshore or streambank or along an animal trail
  - a game or bear trail can often be identified by height, appearing tunnel-like; do not pitch your tent near such as a passage because bears may use it regularly
- position your sleeping area with a clear escape route from a bear, in the open away from dense brush, streams and game trails
  - if pitching a group of tents, form a line, with the tents spaced at least 10 m (33 ft) apart, rather than a circle so that if a bear comes by, it will not feel surrounded

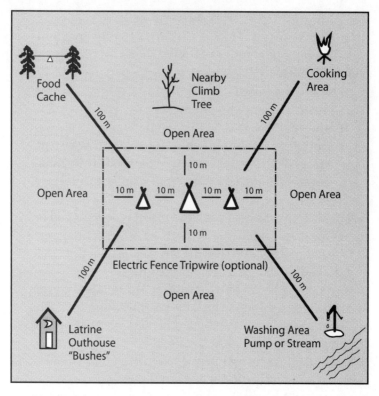

- hang objects around your tent with properties that may deter bears, such as things that have bright or reflective colours or that make noise or flap in wind
- position your cooking, storage and human waste (latrine) areas at a distance from your tenting areas; ensure that when you are using these areas, you always have a clear escape route from a bear
- keep a clean campsite; do not leave food scraps, food containers, garbage, toiletries or other attractants, such as fuels or other aromatic items, lying around
- to reduce attractants, do not bring too many toiletries when camping, and do not keep them in your tent; any of the following may have enough scent to attract a bear (choose unscented products where possible)

- o lip gloss
- o make-up
- o deodorant or antiperspirant
- o perfume
- o soaps, shampoos, etc.
- o creams, lotions and ointments
- o used toothbrushes
- o toothpaste (do not brush your teeth near your tent, the used toothpaste is an attractant; wash away spittings with sufficient water or dry and disperse them with dirt or sand)
- be aware that sunscreens and insect repellents can be attractants; avoid those with heavily scented perfumes; note that citronella (in skin products as well as candles) can be a bear attractant
- properly dispose of used sanitary products with the same protocols described for dealing with other garbage and wastes in camping situations (see facing page)
- leave your pack outside your tent
- consider leaving tent flaps open to permit fast exit
- avoid wandering about at night if possible
- o use a flashlight if you need to go somewhere in the dark
- always supervise small children

Work Camp Safety
- place skirting around all raised structures, including steps, to keep bears from crawling under them
- bears are often attracted to synthetic materials and have been known to eat or chew on inflatable boats, gas cans, sleeping bags, tents, motor oil and seats—if possible, remove such equipment or store it in a location that is inaccessible to bears
- carry a handheld radio when working in the field
- if approaching a work area from the air, check for bears before landing

- work in pairs; take turns watching for bears while your partner works and vice versa
- avoid wandering about at night if possible
  - o use a flashlight if you need to go somewhere in the dark

Camp Cooking, Food Safety and Dealing with Garbage and Food Scraps

- reduce or eliminate odours from yourself, your camp, your clothes and your vehicle
- especially in the backcountry, avoid bringing pungent foods, such as meat and fish; bring freeze-dried foods if possible because they have less odour
- cook and store your food at least 100 m (110 yd) downwind from your campsite
- never cook, eat or store food—including snacks and chewing gum—in your tent
  - o in case of inclement weather, use a tarp for sheltering a separate cooking and eating area
- when cooking, wear a hat or kerchief so your hair does not accumulate odours

- reuse extra cooking grease right away or store it in an airtight container
- pack leftovers in airtight containers with the rest of your food supplies
- wash used cooking and eating utensils, storage containers and tin cans immediately after use
  - wash dishes in fast-moving water of streams or rivers; be aware of bears up- and downstream; or
  - wash dishes in a washing container and dispose of dishwater at least 100 m (110 yd) downwind from your campsite
    - ⊙ use a pit for greasy dishwater and treat with lime or bleach to mask odours
    - ⊙ if you don't have lime or bleach, ensure the pit is about 30 cm (12 in) deep and mix the residue with the substrate while burying
  - have one person on bear lookout while someone is on washing duty
- do not burn large food scraps or garbage in your fire pit—they seldom burn completely and may still attract bears
  - ensure that smaller scraps and fat drippings are thoroughly incinerated
- do not bury food or garbage
  - if you are in a heavily used park area, bear-proof garbage bins are usually provided
  - if you are in the backcountry, contain as best you can any odours from your garbage and pack it out
- store food in airtight containers, a plastic bear-proof container, a plastic-lined duffel bag or a heavy plastic bag, and store the container out of reach of bears; either
  - in the trunk of your car, but only if you have used odour-proof packaging; bears have been known to break in if they smell food, or

- o at least 100 m (110 yd) from your campsite, hanging between two trees several metres apart from each other and at least 4 m (13 ft) above the ground (see Caching Techniques, p. 210)
- cups, containers and pots may retain the odour of coffee, juice or food—properly cache anything that has been in contact with food and do not keep any such item near your tent
- in long-term camps, store food inside locking steel trunks or in sealed metal drums; refrigerators and freezers need be fitted with locks
- do not sleep in clothes that you have worn while cooking food; store cooking clothes as you would your food and toiletries
- if a bear does gain access to your food, garbage or cosmetics
  - o do not try to reclaim these objects from the bear; immediately and calmly leave the area
  - o if you are near a warden's office, all members of the party should leave the campsite and seek assistance
  - o after the bear has gone, your group's safety remains your priority, and the cleanup of debris in the

backcountry is best left until you can return with the authorities; however, if you are still in the area and you need essential supplies and equipment that remain, keep someone on lookout for the bear's possible return as you gather them, then leave the area

o if you are in a recreational or residential area, warn other people nearby and report the bear to authorities

o in a work situation, keep vigilant for the return of the bear and use deterrents—if the bear becomes an ongoing nuisance, report it to the nearest department of natural resources or wildlife authorities

Pet, Horse and Other Animal Safety

- handle, store and remove pet food in camp environments with as much care as you do your own food
- properly dispose of pet wastes (as with human waste, bury it far from campsites and trails) or pack it out
- most backcountry horse-riders do not carry in feed, but in larger trail riding operations, the outfitter should know how to properly store horse feed to avoid bear tampering
- clean up any feed spills
- keep your pet on a leash or inside your vehicle (keep a window slightly open for air, particularly in hot weather)
- dogs should be well trained and well controlled when in bear country; dogs used for protection against bears should be properly trained for this specific skill to understand the difference between deterring and harassing a bear
- although horses may be spooked by bears, making them hard to control, some people say that bears steer clear of llamas

Cottage, Cabin and Residential (Rural and Suburban) Safety

- plan bear awareness meetings with neighbours to implement policies and procedures to avoid attracting bears; consider bear hazards in development plans within or near green spaces (do not plan to build a playground right next to a forest edge, for example)
- make your cottage or cabin as bear-proof as possible
  o use minimum 19 mm ($\frac{3}{4}$") plywood or tongue-and-groove 50 × 800 mm (2 × 8 in) lumber for walls
  o install windows near building exits so people can check for bears before going outside
  o use minimum 50 mm (2 in) lumber for shutters over windows and doors; alternatively, bolt on chain-link fencing or metal grates if you don't have shutters
  o ensure there is no space for a bear to get a claw under a shutter, door or window, by which the bear might be able to pry it open

- o board up doors and windows if leaving for long periods—"bear boards" with protruding nails are sometimes effective
- • maintain a bear-safe yard and garden
  - o keep your lawn mowed and weeded—tall grass and dandelions in flower are attractive to bears
  - o do not use bloodmeal or fish-based products to fertilize your lawn or garden
  - o use electric fencing to protect valuable trees, orchards, vegetable and berry patches (see Fences amd Barriers, p. 211)
    - ⊙ tuber and root vegetables (such as potatoes, carrots and beets) in gardens can attract bears
    - ⊙ certain flowers (such as sweetvetch, dandelion and clover) can attract bears
    - ⊙ bears are particularly attracted to apples, plums, oaks and cherries when in season
  - o pick all ripe fruit off trees
  - o remove vegetables and fallen fruit from the ground
  - o fill birdfeeders only through winter—not from April through November, when birds have ample wild food sources; bears have been shown to be highly attracted to this dependable high-protein source of food
  - o do not leave pet food outdoors
  - o turn off kitchen exhaust fans that vent to the outside when not in use and ensure that the vent screen is cleaned regularly
  - o thoroughly clean outdoor barbecue grills after use
    - ⊙ remove any grease or collection of drippings after each use
    - ⊙ burn off any food residue
    - ⊙ use an ammonia-based cleaner on grills to remove any food odours
    - ⊙ store barbeques or at least the grills in a secured garage or shed

- ⊙ use a barbeque cover and wrap grills in plastic to further mask food odours
- o consider materials that are easiest to clean when planning to construct a barbeque pit or open grill; for example, lava rocks are much more difficult to clean than are bricks, and ceramic bricks are even easier to clean
- • maintain a bear-safe compost
- o do not put meat, fish, grease, oil or dairy products in your compost
- o keep composters as scent-free as possible; turn the contents often and apply lime
- o consider not composting sweet foods, such as fruit, or keep your compost barricaded in some way
- o consider using an indoor worm composter
- • maintain bear-safe garbage
- o if possible, keep garbage securely behind closed doors in a garage, basement or storage area, particularly during early spring and late fall
- o use bear-resistant garbage containers in secured or fenced areas

⊙ request that the municipality or county install bear-proof containers for community parks and streets

o double-bag garbage to reduce odours

o clean garbage containers regularly with bleach or ammonia and place camphor disks or mothballs in the bin to mask odours

o keep meat scraps in the freezer until garbage pickup day; grease, fat, bacon and other pungent meats should be disposed of in sealed containers

o do not leave dirty diapers or diaper pails outside

o rinse all food containers before disposing or recycling

o if your wastewater does not flow into a sewer, septic system or holding tank, clean the exit area of your drain to contain flushed food particles in dishwater

o put garbage out for collection on the morning of pickup—not the night before

o avoid stockpiling garbage, which is a sure way to attract bears; if you are responsible for taking your own garbage to a landfill or garbage transfer station, do so often enough to avoid overflow or rotting smells

o do not burn garbage, because the remains may attract bears (they are attracted to burn areas in the wild as well)

Schoolyard Safety

• make sure rural schools implement bear deterrent policies and that they teach proper bear safety to the children

• teach children to

o immediately get inside the school if they see a bear on or around school property when playing outside and to tell the first adult they see

o never approach a bear

- back away from a nearby bear toward the school and yell at the bear in a voice loud enough that other people will hear and come to help
- drop their backpack if it contains food
- keep lunches indoors
- never leave food, food wrappers or food containers in the schoolyard

Farming Safety

- develop a network with your neighbours to help keep each other informed about bears in your area
- clear or remove any heavy brush surrounding crop production areas
- use electric fencing around orchards, beehives, vegetables and berry patches or between grain crops and adjacent forest areas; install fencing before bears become problematic—electric fencing works only if it is operating before bears become food conditioned
- pick all ripe fruit off trees and remove vegetables and fallen fruit from the ground
- cereal crops such as wheat, oats and barely can attract bears—be cautious when working or walking around crops
- clean up any spilled grain
- locate granaries and storage facilities away from homes, children's play areas or other areas frequented by people
  - granaries should be well-maintained and of sturdy construction
- keep livestock away from forests and bear travel routes
- keep heavily pregnant cows within electric fencing to prevent attack while giving birth or predation on the newborns
- ensure that your calving area is located in an open space away from forest cover

- keep calves in a protected lot or corral until they are at least 3–4 weeks old and do not place them in remote fields until they are 6 months; their small size and their inquisitive and non-defensive nature make them easy prey
- because bears may target sick or injured animals, keep livestock confined in a bear-safe area for at least 10 days after castration, dehorning or branding
- salt and mineral blocks set out for livestock or to attract deer can also attract bears, so be attentive as to where you place them
- bears are the most active at dusk and dawn—semi-confinement of sheep at night will reduce predation
- dispose of animal carcasses in a timely manner
  o avoid burying carcasses; if necessary, bury them under at least 1.2 m (4 ft) of soil covered with lime
  o avoid burning carcasses or food waste, which may attract bears; if burning is necessary, do so far away from working and residential areas
- immediately report livestock depredation
- if you shoot a bear, contact your local conservation office by the next business day

ADDITIONAL AVOIDANCE TECHNIQUES
AGAINST GRIZZLIES

Although all the above avoidance techniques are applicable to both black bears and grizzly bears, there are additional considerations when in grizzly bear territory.

Avoid grizzly feeding areas, including floodplains, berry patches, recent burns, wet meadows, avalanche slopes, alpine meadows and streams or rivers where fish are spawning. Where possible, keep a safe distance when walking alongside dense brush. Avoid walking through heavy brush, where bears can be eating, caching prey or sleeping. If you need to walk through dense brush, make lots of noise. Avoid alder thickets, where a high frequency of attacks has occurred.

Grizzlies and black bears both scratch, bite or rub on trees to mark their territory, but grizzly scratch marks can be recognized by their greater depth, length and breadth. You can gauge how recently marks to a tree have been made by seeing whether the wood looks freshly exposed or has a dried scar.

If you come across a dug-up area, it is likely the work of a grizzly bear. These diggings can be very large and be formed from multiple digs. To determine whether the bear is still in the area or has likely moved on, cautiously investigate how recently the digging occurred. If the vegetation that has had dirt strewn on top of it is still green and living, it was recently covered, whereas yellowed vegetation has likely been covered for a while. If the bear was digging roots, see if the remains of the roots are still fresh or if they are dried or wilting.

If you come across a digging that is more of a mound of dirt and vegetation, you may have found where a grizzly has cached (buried) its prey—black bears do not excavate for this purpose, although they often drag their prey into a hidden or obscure area and simply brush loose dirt and leaf litter over-top. You may also smell the carcass or notice swarms of flies or a large number of crows or ravens around. If you see a "murder" of crows or a large flock of ravens, you may be near a carcass. Leave the area immediately and efficiently, being extremely vigilant because likely the bear is nearby. Avoid drawing attention to yourself until you are far away from the carcass; whereas you would normally want to be noisy to alert a bear of your presence, being near a bear's food cache is never acceptable to the bear, and it may not yet have noticed you.

When tenting in grizzly territory, minimize the number of tents in camp; a few big tents are better than many small ones. Place them in a line or semicircle with enough space between them to allow a bear an easy escape route. Use a tent that is larger than you require because grizzlies, especially food-conditioned grizzlies, have been known to attack tents if they see something brushing along the fabric of the tent wall.

Hunting in grizzly territory introduces many dangers because a hunter's behaviour is contrary to many bear avoid-ance techniques: hunters move quietly through dense brush, easily startling a bear. The biggest risk is when a hunter has shot its quarry, for now the hunter is deliberately hanging around an animal carcass. A report made by Hererro and Higgins ("Human Injuries Inflicted by Bears in Alberta, 1960–98") stated that "50 percent (4/8) of grizzly bear–inflicted injuries on Alberta provincial lands were associated with hunting." The rate of injury in BC was 35 percent (17/49). The report further explains that grizzly bears may claim carcasses of animals shot by hunters and left for a short while and defend those kills as their own. There have been rare cases where a grizzly has even attempted to take an animal carcass away from a hunter. In comparison, there were no cases of black bears demonstrating this behaviour, and no hunters were injured by black bears during this same study period.

It is not easy to recognize bear species by the size of their scat, but that of grizzlies will include slightly different vegetation (roots and tubers); it is more important to identify if the bear, regardless of species, is in the immediate area and if it has been eating meat. If the scat is fresh, it won't have many insects on it yet, and the grass or vegetation it is lying on will still be green, whereas vegetation will be yellowed if the scat is older. Scat from bears that have been feeding only on vegetation will be fibrous or have seeds or bluish-purplish colouring from berries. If the bear was feeding on meat, the scat will be very black and runny, and there may be hair. Carefully leave this area immediately—you do not want to be in the vicinity of a carcass that a bear may be defending.

AVOIDANCE TECHNIQUES AGAINST POLAR BEARS

Many avoidance techniques—such as being alert, properly storing and cooking food, avoiding prey carcasses and making your presence as obvious as possible so as not to sneak up on a bear—apply to any bear. However, the specific habitat conditions in the Arctic as well as the distinct behaviour and biology of polar bears make northern situations with potential for human-bear conflict different than those in the south.

Consider hiring a local guide when travelling in arctic backcountry. Doing so provides employment, increases your safety and gives you the advantage of a local expert who may teach you a few things about the Arctic, offering you a local perspective and insights on the land, the people and the wildlife.

Hired guides are mandatory for sport hunters that are not resident of the territory or province in which the hunt occurs. Other tourists are not required to hire a guide for camping and canoeing, but the tourism agencies of the territories can recommend links and contacts for outfitters and guides that can be privately hired. Hunting guides are recommended based on experience and are hired through tour agencies and private outfitters that sell hunting packages to tourists. Hiring these guides for expeditions not related to hunting is not yet common in Canada but definitely has the potential to grow into a form of ecotourism for the North. Currently, there is no certification process for training to be a guide or for establishing any parameters for the profession, so ask around for someone with a good reputation.

Safety in Polar Bear Country

- learn about polar bear behaviour and habitats
- make sure that every member of your travelling group is familiar with the risks, avoidance techniques and how to deal with an encounter and use the deterrents
- carry some form of deterrent, repellent or weapon (see Deterrents, p. 200)
  - o if traversing or camping in the Arctic, it is highly recommended that you carry and know how to use a firearm; make sure the firearm is capable of stopping a polar bear attack
  - ⊙ carry a firearm only if you know how and when to use it and are licenced to carry it and authorized to use it; a gun with rubber or plastic bullets is also an option; check with Parks Canada staff or government wildlife offices for regulations governing carrying and using firearms
  - o carry flares and use them to scare or distract a bear from continuing to advance on you; shoot them upward to arc forward and land in front of the bear
  - ⊙ practice shooting flares before embarking on any trek
- do not travel alone through polar bear country; travel with at least one other person
- travel with a dog, but only if it has proven experience with polar bears; keep dogs under control at all times
- travel in daylight if at all possible
- stay alert; scan your surroundings frequently with binoculars
- avoid high drifts, ice walls or cliffs where ambush is a possibility
- make noise while hiking in polar bear territory to avoid sneaking up on and surprising a polar bear

- be wary around open water where a polar bear can suddenly emerge
- move quickly, quietly and warily away from any mammal carcasses you may encounter; never approach any animal carcass
- watch for tracks, droppings or dens
- do not get between a female and her cubs
- stay at least 100 m (110 yd) away from polar bears; do not approach polar bears for any reason, no matter how good the photo might be
- if in a vehicle, even a Tundra Buggy or similar bear-watching vehicle, keep your arms and head inside and not hanging out the windows

Camping Safety

- consider bringing and setting up a portable tripwire or motion detector system to alert you if a polar bear approaches your camp; it may be worth it, particularly for a semi-permanent camp
  - make sure every member of your group knows how to operate the system
  - set up a periphery at least 10 m (33 ft) from the tents to give time to grab a rifle or other deterrent
- avoid setting up campsites on beaches and along the coast, especially in fall; the least likely time of year for polar bears to hunt is in summer, a period of natural fasting, but, starting in October, they begin searching for prey and are at their most dangerous
- avoid camping in areas prone to ambush or along the natural bear pathways—below ledges, cliffs or over-hangs, near large snowdrifts or in narrow valleys or passes
- camp in areas of high visibility, inland on high ground
- when choosing a campsite, scan the area with binoculars; ensure your range of view all around you is long and clear; scout for bear tracks, droppings or

dens in the immediate area—at least 100–150 m (110–165 yd) in all directions—to include the areas to be used for caching food, latrines, cooking, washing and so on

- if practical, camp in a large group—more people may deter a bear, or if it could not be detterred, more people will be available to fend off an attack or provide care or seek help for anyone injured
- position your camping, cooking, storage and human waste (latrine) areas so that you always have a clear escape route from any approaching bear
- in the backcountry, always sleep in a tent, not in the open
- consider taking patrol shifts throughout the night
- tie dogs downwind from your sleeping area
- keep a clean campsite; do not leave food scraps, food containers, garbage, toiletries or other attractants, such as fuels or other aromatic items, lying around
- do not bring pungent foods (such as meat or fish) with you
- store and cook food at least 100 m (110 yd) from your tent
- store and clean pots, stoves, utensils, etc. at least 100 m (110 yd) from your tent
- store scented products and the clothing you were wearing while cooking at least 100 m (110 yd) from your tent; when cooking, wear a hat or kerchief to avoid having your hair accumulate odours
- use storage containers that are bear-proof, airtight or both
- pack out your garbage and food scraps to avoid bears becoming habituated to humans as food sources
- if you are not willing to pack out your feces, as recommended by experts, bury wastes under rocks, away from the trail, at least 100 m (110 yd) from your camp and away from all water sources; put all used toilet

paper and feminine hygiene products in a sealed bag with your garbage and pack it out

- clean up dog food leftovers and pack them out along with dog feces
- do not burn any garbage or food scraps
- if camping in a cabin or trailer, consider how to reduce the odours within your living space, abiding by the same rules as if you were tenting; ensure that the entrances to the cabin or trailer are secure but that you have an escape route if a bear manages to enter

Deterrents

Don't wait for an actual attack to try out the technical deterrents you have purchased and brought along with you. There is no guarantee that any of these deterrents or weapons will be effective or function properly in an emergency situation; research well the various options available to you and make your own best judgement based on what you trust and what you are comfortable employing.

Learn how to use all weapons, even flare guns and rifles with rubber bullets; do not rely on assumed skills. With firearms and pepper spray, it might be fun to set up a target practice with friends who are also interested in learning bear defence skills (use a firing range or other safe area for practicing with bullets). Set up standard targets as well as moving (charging) targets for various challenges that simulate a real bear encounter. Be aware of the challenges in using deterrents against a moving object and with wind or other environmental impediments and in performing these skills with speed.

The availability of commercial bear deterrents such as bear spray, noisemakers and flares is limited in the Arctic. Therefore, most deterrents must be purchased elsewhere and transported (often as dangerous goods).

BEAR SPRAY (ALSO KNOWN AS PEPPER SPRAY)

Carry bear spray and know how to use it. There are many bear spray manufacturers; when selecting a product from the various options, ensure that the can contains at least 225 g (7.9 oz)—260 g (9 oz) is typical—with a minimum 0.85 percent concentration of capsaicin. The natural ingredient oleoresin capsicum is only a deterrent at close range; the active ingredient in oleoresin capsicum, capsaicin, is an oil-like resin derived from cayenne pepper that is responsible for the burning sensation derived from the spray. Under typical conditions, range is good up to 6–7 m (20–23 ft), but it is most effective at 3–4 m (10–13 ft).

Read the label carefully and be sure that the product you choose contains the minimum content of the active ingredient and that the product is labelled as a deterrent and not as a repellent. It should have a shelf life of four years and be registered as a product under the Pest Controls Product Act. The label should also state the spray duration, which needs to be a minimum of six seconds. Choose a spray that dispenses the contents in a wide rather than a narrow stream, to increase your target success.

Carry two canisters per person; one within easy reach and the second as a replacement if you have used the first one and still need to hike for several days. At the very least, carry one canister per person with at least one extra canister within the group for replacement in the field. Carry the bear spray canister where it is easily accessible, preferably in a holster on a belt or backpack.

If a bear is spotted at close range—within 100 m (110 yd) is already too close for comfort—have the bear spray in hand and ready to use if necessary. If the bear comes within 6–7 m (20–23 ft), this is the maximum distance that the spray will be effective, and you can consider using it—remove the safety clip; within 3–4 m (10–13 ft), it is definitely time to use the spray. To employ the spray, depress the trigger with your thumb and hold it down for a 2–3 second burst of spray directly into the bear's face. To be effective, the spray must hit the eyes and nose of the bear. The spray will be released from the canister in a wide fog. The engaged canister will make a sudden, loud hissing with the release of the spray, which sometimes also startles the bear into stopping its approach or backing off. Observe the bear's reaction to each assault of the spray and do not empty the can in one go because you may need to fire at the bear more than once. After use, replace bear spray as soon as possible because a single use can deplete up to half of the contents. In a situation where bear spray may save your life, you want a full canister at your disposal.

Do not spray with the wind in your face, or you will spray yourself instead of the bear. When discharging the spray, take short, shallow breaths as a precaution to minimize how much you might accidentally inhale. In both bears and humans, bear spray can cause difficulty breathing, is inflammatory and is an extreme irritant to the eyes, possibly causing acute blindness. The effects are temporary, but the painful and debilitating symptoms can last up to an hour; if the symptoms persist, seek medical attention. If a person's skin comes in contact with the spray, wash the affected areas with plenty of cool, clean water for about 15 minutes. If eyes are affected, remove contact lenses and flush eyes for about 15 minutes. If inhalation has seriously hampered or stopped the person from breathing, move to an area of fresh air, give artificial respiration and seek medical attention.

Immediately, and carefully, remove and either pack contaminated clothing in an airtight bag or thoroughly wash all clothing, including shoes, that has come into contact with the spray, first because you want to avoid further possibility of skin problems, and second because the diluted scent of the liquid can be interpreted as a food aroma by bears. Suggested products to wash off capsaicin include soap or shampoo but also oils such as vegetable oil, paraffin or petroleum jelly or products such as vinegar, bleach or topical antacid suspensions

(Alka-seltzer can be used to treat bites and stings as well as irritation from bear spray and also has cleaning properties). Because bear spray can act as an attractant in mild concentrations, do not spray it on clothing, tents or any other items in the hope of keeping bears away—unlike bug repellent, bear spray is useful only as a deterrent applied directly to the bear.

Bear spray is not a substitute for practicing bear awareness and safety, and it is not guaranteed to deter a bear or protect against injury in an attack. The most difficult aspect of using bear spray is maintaining calm; because the bear is at such close range and perhaps approaching quickly, remaining calm is extremely difficult but crucial in order to be able to judge wind direction. Don't wait until an encounter to practice using bear spray for the first time. Prior to entering bear country, know how to discharge a can by actually discharging one. There are "inert training canisters" on the market, made specifically for practice purposes. Being able to quickly draw the canister from a holster and remove the safety is the first required skill; knowing how to aim by judging the wind and distance is the next critical skill.

A bear hit with the spray may be only temporarily deterred, so you should immediately leave the area after the bear encounter. Do not re-use partially discharged canisters, but put them in an airtight bag because the smell can actually attract bears. Carry an extra can in case of malfunction or the unlikely event of having more than one encounter during your travels.

Bear spray may work on polar bears but has not been thoroughly tested. It is known that one Japanese polar trekker in Norway effectively used bear spray to deter a polar bear.

Be aware that bear spray may not work when it is cold or wet, so try it beforehand in the conditions in which you anticipate using it. Do not store bear spray above 50° C (122° F) or below 10° C (50° F).

Keep the can close at hand and inside your sleeping bag at night. Ensure that the safety clip is on the trigger when the canister is being stored or carried. It is recommended that you keep bear spray canisters out of the passenger or operator compartment when in a vehicle, aircraft, boat or other transportation or heavy operational equipment to avoid having an accidental discharge of the spray seriously handicap the operator. Check the list of prohibited items before planning to bring bear spray onto a commercial flight. For small planes, check with the pilot before bringing bear spray onboard. Store the spray in an airtight container away from heat sources.

Compared to all other deterrents, bear spray, when properly used, has statistically shown to be the best method of defence against a bear attack and for preventing injury to both person and bear.

FIREARMS

No deterrent or response to an attack is guaranteed to stop or prevent human injury by an attacking bear. The use of a firearm to deal with a dangerous bear is always a last resort, and it may not even be an option in regulated areas. Many parks (national, provincial or otherwise) do not allow the use of firearms, and handguns are restricted in Canada; therefore, ample research is required not only to operate your firearms responsibly but also not to break the law. Bears are protected as big game species, and shooting a bear—even on your own private property—may be illegal if you did not follow the proper protocols with the appropriate conservation departments.

Have the proper licence to acquire, carry and use any firearms you plan to bring, and know the jurisdictions in which carrying a gun is legal. You must have the proper training and a possession-and-acquisition licence (PAL) and have the gun registered with the federal government; provinces and territories may have specific regulations in addition to federal regulations. For example, people coming to camp in polar bear territory in Nunavut can bring a gun for self-defence; however, if a bear is killed, issues will arise with the nearest community because the bear will be removed from a strictly monitored quota, thereby resulting in one less hunting opportunity, which can potentially be an economic loss. More information on firearms is available from the RCMP through the Canada Firearms Centre: http://www.cfc-cafc.gc.ca/

Make sure that you know how to use the firearm, that it is in good condition and that it is clean and ready for immediate use. It takes discipline and ability to use a gun conscientiously; know how and when to shoot. Rifles kick hard and take practice and strength to use properly.

If you know how to use a gun, are licenced to carry it and are mentally prepared to use it to defend your life or that of one of your companions against a bear if necessary, make sure that you are armed with a firearm that is capable of stopping a bear attack. If you do not understand the power of the firearm and ammunition necessary to kill a bear, you may only injure it, which is not only inhumane but also potentially more dangerous. A 12-gauge shotgun or a .30-06 calibre rifle loaded with heavy slugs is perhaps the best and easiest to use at close range to kill any bear.

Bring ample ammunition, which hopefully will never have to be used as other than a noise-making deterrent; know how many cartridges or shells you have loaded and always keep the gun loaded. Never allow all the ammunition to be exhausted even when firing as deterrent—you don't want to run out of ammunition when the bullet may have to save your life. Treat every firearm as if it is loaded, even if it is not. Never shoot at hard surfaces or water. Never climb, run or jump with a loaded firearm.

In the Arctic, keep your gun outside the tent—inside, it will ice up—but tie a string to it leading into the tent for easy access in an emergency or in the dark. Protect the gun in canvas wrapped in durable plastic to keep moisture out, and in a padded gun cover with a shoulder strap. Carry it with you at all times (do not leave it on the sled). Mantle and test fire occasionally. Be familiar with the gun and whether it has a history of any malfunction.

There are specific laws and regulations in each province and territory about how to deal with a bear carcass. For example, if conservation authorities cannot be contacted to deal with the carcass, you may be responsible by law to skin and preserve the hide and skull or lower jaw, even in a self-defence kill.

Choosing to carry a gun comes with the responsibility of knowing how to use it effectively and safely. Practice with moving targets and have an almost instinctual comfort loading and firing a gun so that under situations of duress (a bear attack may offer only mere seconds in which to respond), you'll be able to do what you have to do. People with experience in these situations can hold their ground until a bear is within 4.5 m (15 ft); inexperienced shooters will tend to fire at a bear at much greater distance, when a bear may only be bluff charging and, if so, typically stops short at this 4.5 m (15 ft) line. For the reason of close range, pepper spray is often considered to be more appropriate and does not result in killing or injuring the bear.

Different types of rifles and pistols can be used as various forms of bear deterrent. A large bear rifle with heavy ammunition is a lethal weapon, but other guns can shoot lethal bullets as well as non-lethal rubber bullets, blanks as a noisemaker or even flares.

12-gauge Beanbags, Rubber Buckshot and Rubber Slugs

Beanbags, rubber buckshot and rubber slugs are all physical deterrents available as non-lethal shotgun rounds. The beanbag is a 2.5-cm (1-in) fabric bag filled with lead shot. The maximum effective range is 25 m (80 ft), and it should not be fired at a bear that is closer than 5 m (16 ft). The rubber buckshot consists of rubber balls similar in size to 00 buckshot.

The maximum effective range is 30 m (100 ft), and it should not be fired at a bear within 5 m (16 ft). The rubber slug is a 73-grain rubber baton. Its maximum effective range is 75 m (245 ft), and it should not to be fired at a bear within 8 m (26 ft). Aim for the hindquarters of the bear, never the head. Any of the preceding rounds should be used only in shotguns with barrels that are not "choked" (restricted to control pellet spread). Ensure a clear line of fire and avoid obstacles that could invite ricochets.

Shooting a rubber bullet at a bear has proven to be a good deterrent in some situations. Moreover, rubber bullets are legal, whereas shooting to kill a bear without first trying to deter it, especially at long range, may result in criminal charges. However, a bear that already perceives you as a threat may be further angered by your hostility in firing rubber bullets or even warning shots. A bear injured by a trajectory of any kind may likely become more aggravated and thus an even more dangerous bear.

Flares

Carry an overly sufficient supply; the technique used by Helen Thayer (see story, p. 165) was to fire a sort of wall or barricade of flares between her and the bear; bears may avoid walking close to or over a burning element. Flares can ignite fires in dry areas and should not be used where the risk of forest fire is high. Some kinds of flares are fired from a gun and others are not.

Noise Deterrents

Starter pistols firing blanks, pen-launched "bear bangers" and loud whistles or "screamers" are forms of noisemakers that can be effective in scaring off bears, and they are relatively easy to use, but they may be prohibited in certain areas, so always inquire with local conservation offices or the RCMP.

A pen launcher is a pen-like device that fires a bear banger. The 15-mm banger has a .22 calibre blank that is screwed into the pen and fired; it travels approximately 30 m (100 ft) and explodes in a loud bang. These pen launchers can also fire signal flares. The flight pattern is direct and consistent.

Another form of banger is a 15-mm cartridge that can be fired from a .22 calibre rifle. This banger also travels about 30 m (100 ft) and explodes with a loud bang.

A screamer is a type of noise deterrent that is also a 15-mm cartridge fired from a .22 rifle. When fired, it emits a continuous screaming noise for approximately 100 m (110 yd) as it follows with an erratic flight pattern.

Also available are 12-gauge crackers and 12-gauge whistle crackers, which are loaded into 12-gauge shotguns (unchoked to prevent barrel obstruction); when fired, they travel about 100 m (110 yd) and explode with a loud bang or emit a long, screeching whistle before exploding. The flight patterns are consistent. Check for blockages in the barrel of the shotgun after the use of these crackers.

These gun-fired bangers can injure people and must be used with caution. Be sure you have a clear line of fire without obstacles that could cause ricochet. They can also ignite fires in dry areas and should not be used where the risk of forest fire is high.

Do not shoot the deterrent at the bear. Aim for a point in between the bear and yourself (or the person under threat) so that it explodes in front of the bear and causes it to flee away from you and your companions.

BEAR DOGS

Keep dogs away from bears unless they are properly bear-trained animals. There are examples of poorly trained dogs that have irritated a bear or enticed it to follow, leading the bear to their owner (see stories, pp. 60 & 110). Always keep dogs tied or on a leash when in bear territory. Many parks and agencies of public lands within bear territory discourage the presence of dogs, which can increase rather than decrease the chance of a bear encounter—as well as harass other wild-life and possibly annoy other people.

However, a well-trained dog can save a person from a bear attack by deterring or distracting the bear so that the person can escape. The disposition of the dog is important; the dog must understand boundaries and not seek out bears, harass or taunt them. The dog must have the ability to work effectively with a nuisance bear and yet not have an aggressive personality around people or other animals. The dog must be able to shepherd or deter the bear rather than simply annoy it. Medium-sized dogs are best suited to bear work, having a large enough presence to threaten a bear while still being agile, fast, quick of reflex and energetic. Border collies, heelers and shepherds are recognized, but spitz breeds, such as huskies, laikas and Karelians, are best.

Karelian bear dogs have been bred over hundreds of years to work with bears. They require an experienced owner and handler. In 2001, Alberta Fish and Wildlife launched a four-year pilot program in collaboration with the Wind River Bear Institute (www.beardogs.org). At the time of publication of this book, four Karelian bear dogs were "on staff" in Cochrane and the Crowsnest Pass area. Alberta is the first jurisdiction in Canada to employ bear dogs, which have proven to be effective in augmenting bear behaviour through "intensive bear shepherding" in high bear-human density areas such as campgrounds, residential areas and other locations where bear presence is unacceptable. The bears are hazed with the dogs and rubber bullets to reinforce a negative association with humans, and the hazing ceases once the bears have returned to their appropriate territory. The dogs are also used in first-response situations to track reported nuisance bears and other wildlife, including cougars, bighorn sheep and moose, and they assist conservation officers in dealing with the food caches of bear kills in human activity areas or tracking carcasses of poached bears.

The use of bear dogs to deter bears from human-occupied areas has been shown to have long-term effectiveness in conditioning bears to understand what areas they should not enter, resulting in less damage to property, less injury to humans and, especially, less bears being destroyed. This innovative program hopefully marks a transition from the costly—and often unsuccessful—approach of relocating nuisance bears. BC has now started its own pilot program, and likely other provinces will soon follow suit.

CACHING TECHNIQUES

Store food in airtight containers at least 100 m (110 yd) away from the tenting area and at least 5 m (16 ft) high between two trees (see illustration). If you are in a treeless area, use airtight metal drums and store them 100 m (110 yd) away from the tenting area.

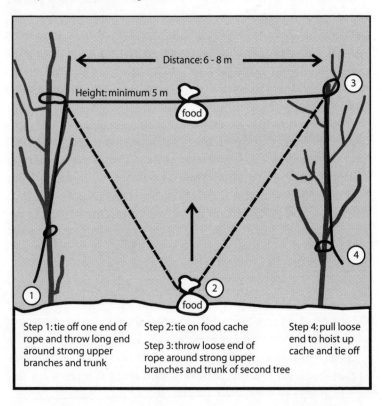

Distance: 6 - 8 m

Height: minimum 5 m

food

3

4

1

2

food

Step 1: tie off one end of rope and throw long end around strong upper branches and trunk

Step 2: tie on food cache

Step 3: throw loose end of rope around strong upper branches and trunk of second tree

Step 4: pull loose end to hoist up cache and tie off

BEAR BELLS AND WHISTLES

There is controversy today over the effectiveness of bells and whistles. Some people contend that habituated bears associate the bells with humans and their food. Some experts also argue that whistles may mimic the distress calls of young ungulates or other small animals, which may attract bears looking for prey.

FENCES AND BARRIERS

Given the opportunity, both grizzlies and black bears prey on cattle, sheep and other livestock, and the black bear's fondness for honey is infamous. Electric fences can be installed around livestock lots or apiaries permanently or temporarily. A bear that is attracted to the fence or what the fence is guarding will investigate with its nose and quickly receive a painful shock that will cause it to flee. The negative experience will not be forgotten; bears that have come into contact with an electric fence in the past will likely be deterred from this or a similar fence in the future without having to investigate again.

To deter a bear, the fence must have at least four or five wires electrified in pulses of about 40 per minute—NOT in a steady charge. The wires should start at 15 cm (6 in) above the ground and continue in equal increments to 1 m (3 ft) in height. If the wires are spaced wider or higher off the ground, the bear will be able to get its head through before being shocked, and a shock to the face is the most effective deterrent. The lower the wire the better, as bears are not inclined to jump or even step over the fence. The tighter the wire spacing, the more of a deterrent to the bear. Wire with metal wires interwoven with polywire is recommended. The easiest approach for non-experts is to build a system with alternating hot and ground wires. This system reduces most of the operator difficulties in fence design and use.

Proper grounding is a must. A galvanized metal ground rod 1.2–2 m (4–7 ft) long, pounded into the ground with only about 15 cm (6 in) emerging aboveground and attached to the ground terminal of the fence charger should suffice, but a series of up to three, spaced in a row about 3 m (10 ft) apart is better. This grounding will ensure that the bear receives a shock because its heavily padded feet may conduct the charge into the ground. Most bear fence models meet 6000-volt and 0.7-joule specifications. Depending on your needs, choose a 12-volt portable system, with a 12-volt deep cycle marine battery connected to an appropriately sized solar panel to keep the battery charged (check with the supplier, because the best choice will depend on the average amount of sunlight in the place it will be used), or a 110-volt AC power system. Keep wires taunt and knots at insulators tight. Trim grass and other vegetation around the fence to keep it from touching the wire and draining the charge.

If your fence is meant to guard a calving or lambing yard, you might want to have a second, unelectrified barrier fence on the inside of the electric fence, both to avoid shocking young animals and to prevent them from lying near the fence within reach of a bear.

Straps around apiaries in addition to electric fencing are recommended; do not place apiaries near a stream, game trail, forest edge or garbage or compost site. There are very detailed and useful instructions on how to install electric fences around apiaries on the Manitoba government's conservation website at www.gov.mb.ca/conservation/wildlife/problem_wildlife/bbear_fence.html

Electric fencing around a long-term or short-term campsite or around game caches from hunting does not require the heavy infrastructure that is required around livestock; systems for camping weigh as little as 4.5 kg (10 lb) including poles, wire, charger and grounding rods and can be set up in about half an hour. There is also net fencing on the market that looks similar to a volleyball net with strands of stainless steel and polyethylene wire.

Tripwires and alarms are easiest to employ in small camping areas, which are arguably in greater need of protection anyway. Lightweight and portable, they are useful in a mobile camping situation. Some kinds of alarms detect motion or infrared heat, but tripwire alarms that use an electrical wire around the camp perimeter, with an alarm that is triggered if the wire is touched or broken, are most common. The lightweight wire can be strung with simple tent poles, sticks or other makeshift posts. Although the sound of an alarm may not deter a bear, it will give the camp's occupants warning to respond to the situation and use more effective deterrents. In areas of high bear densities, these systems offer peace of mind and a good night's sleep.

BEAR-PROOF GARBAGE AND COMPOST BINS

Two sources for purchasing bear-proof containers are
- www.bearsaver.com/ResidentialPolyCarts.htm
- www.bearproofcontainers.com

You can also choose to construct your own bearproof containers or barriers around garbage bins and composters. Bolting together 5 × 15 cm (2 × 6 in) boards around the bin along with a securely fastened lid may be adequate, although even this level of security is not guaranteed against a determined bear. Help to avoid surprise human-bear encounters by keeping garbage storage bins in open areas with good visibility. Also, regardless of how secure the container is, do what you reasonably can to keep aromas to a minimum.

Emergency Situations

Bring a first aid kit with you into backcountry situations. Include the following essential items in the kit: a syringe, saline and antiseptic such as iodine for cleaning wounds (bear bites and scratches have a great deal of bacteria); plenty of sterile bandages, dressings, gauze and tapes; and an emergency rescue blanket and heat packs.

Two recommended wilderness first aid certification and training organizations in Canada are Sirius Wilderness Medicine (www.siriusmed.com) and Slipstream First Aid (www.wildernessfirstaid.ca). Useful books include *Medicine for the Outdoors*, by Paul Auerbach, and *NOLS Wilderness First Aid*, by Tod Schimelpfenig and Linda Lindsey. In addition, the Wilderness Medical Society publishes practice guidelines.

If a person has been attacked by a bear, keep the victim warm and conscious—continue to talk to him or her in a calm, reassuring manner.

Do not leave a victim behind when you go for help unless you have no other choice; if you find anybody else in the area, ask them to seek help for you and then return to the victim.

Ideally, you will be carrying a Personal Locator Beacon (PLB) that will relay your location coordinates to dispatch an emergency response search and rescue. These devices can be purchased at outdoor recreational gear retailers.

In an immediate emergency, contact your local police force or dial 911.

To report bear problems such as a bear in your yard, in the area, at a dump or local garbage drop-off or any other situation that may cause safety concerns, contact the nearest Fish and Wildlife office, Ministry of Natural Resources or Parks and Protected Areas office. Unfortunately, there is no easy toll-free number across the country; each provincial and territorial jurisdiction deals with these reports. Quite often the Report a Poacher number is the same number to call to report a nuisance bear.

- BC: Report a Poacher 1-877-952-7277
- AB: Report a Poacher 1-800-642-3800; Fish and Wildlife 310-0000
- SK: Park Watch 1-800-667-1788; Report a Poacher 1-800-667-7561
- MB: Tip Line 1-800-782-0076; Manitoba Conservation General Information 1-800-214-6497
- ON: Bear Reporting Line 1-866-514-BEAR or 705-945-7641; Report A Poacher 1-800-642-3800
- QC: SOS Braconnage 1-800-463-2191
- NB: no toll-free number; contact the nearest Department of Natural Resources
- NS: Report a Poacher 1-800-565-2224
- NL: no toll-free number; contact the nearest Department of Natural Resources
- NU: there is no toll-free or emergency number and limited infrastructure for telephones and cell phones; the use of two-way radios in the field or knowing the local conservation office telephone number or address may be the only options depending on location. You may be wise to carry an emergency PLB in arctic backcountry.
- NWT: Report a Poacher 1-866-762-2437
- YK: Turn in Poachers 1-800-661-0525

Terminology

altricial: under-developed at birth (or upon hatching), typically meaning blind, hairless and unable to stand or walk (e.g. humans and bears); opposite of precocial (e.g. deer)

behaviour, defensive: the bear is displaying stress from a perceived threat to itself, its cubs or a food source, such as a berry patch or a carcass; often prerequisite to a violent attack

behaviour, offensive: the bear is asserting dominance but not aggression

behaviour, predatory: the bear is displaying casual or intense interest, approaching, following, stalking or circling without any signs of stress

bluff charge: a charge that stops before contact is made; a bluff charge has all the same signs as a real charge, and you won't know whether it is a bluff or real until the moment contact is made or not made.

carnivore: a meat eater, having primarily but not necessarily exclusively a diet of meat

carrion: dead animal matter

cob: cub of the year

compost: decomposing plant matter for use as soil fertilizer and/or to reduce biodegradable organic material entering landfills; may include food scraps, fruits and vegetables, grass clippings, leaves or other organic matter

conditioned (food conditioned): a bear that has had a positive experience by successfully seeking out or preferring unnatural food sources becomes conditioned to human food sources: food stuffs people bring into campgrounds or backcountry, pet food, garbage in campgrounds or residential areas, crops or livestock. The greater the frequency of foraging success on human foods with few negative results, such as hazing, the more conditioned the bear becomes and the more likely that the bear cannot be reconditioned to its natural food sources. Food-conditioned bears typically end up destroyed—a fed bear is a dead bear.

conservation: protection and management of the natural environment, including wildlife, habitat and ecosystems; attempts to mediate human use activities such as recreation activities, residential or industrial development, hunting, agriculture or extractive industry. Preservation aims to remove human impacts from a natural environment, keeping it as pristine as possible for the protection and study of its various components, such as ecosystems, gene pools and wildlife behaviour, to stand as benchmarks to better implement conservation policies.

encounter: the bear and the person are aware of each other's presence; in most encounters, the bear moves away. If the bear is unaware, it is only a bear sighting.

endangered species: listed by the Committee on the Status of Endangered Wildlife in Canada (COSEWIC) as "facing imminent extinction or extirpation." Canada does not have federal endangered species legislation.

extinct: the species no longer exists

extirpated: the species no longer exists in a specified area of its former range, but does exist elsewhere in the wild

habituated: becoming accustomed to human activity and development, including residential, industrial and recreational areas; though retaining a preference to natural food sources, the bear will not be fearful of humans or respond to noise, shouting or hazing from humans. The interactions with humans are either neutral or positive (in the case of food reward), allowing the bear to become more comfortable with human presence. Bears exhibiting nuisance activity by daytime tend to be more highly habituated than bears that seek opportunities at night, a time with which they associate less risk of encounter.

hazing: shouting, throwing rocks or other objects, waving objects, using noise makers, bangers or air horns or shooting with rubber bullets to deter the bear

herbivore: having a diet exclusively comprised of plants

hibernation: a state of dormancy entered during winter; metabolism slows and body temperature falls. Bears are not true hibernators because their body temperatures do not drop and they awake easily; they can temporarily come out of hibernation in warm weather snaps.

leads: open water areas surrounded by sea ice, typically opening and closing (freezing) annually in the same precise location but may be unpredictable

landfast ice: ice near shore and anchored to the ground below the water level either where water depth is less than ice thickness or in deeper water where pressure ridges become grounded; close to shore it is flat, stable. It extends in late winter and spring out to 20 m (60 ft) depths, where it becomes increasingly rough and irregular, and melts in summer, retreating back to land and leaving open water.

montane: a biogeographical zone in mountain regions consisting of high elevation valleys and upland slopes marked by mild temperatures and high precipitation below the treeline of predominantly coniferous forests

omnivore: having a diet comprised of both plants and animals

pack ice: free-floating ice comprised of both the new winter ice and the permanent ice that does not melt. Most of the Polar Ice Cap is pack ice.

polynya: an area where leads persist seasonally and predict-
ably

shear zone: where moving ice hits the seaward edge of landfast ice

stalking: when a bear circles or follows potential prey in a
deliberate, stealth-like manner

threatened species: a species that is at risk of becoming
endangered if factors negatively affecting its population are
not removed or reversed

tundra: a biogeographical zone in the arctic or subarctic
regions consisting of level or undulating treeless plains
with permanently frozen ground where mosses, heaths and
lichens are the dominant vegetation; also referred to as
barren-grounds

ungulate: herbivorous mammal possessing hooves

vulnerable species: a species with a low population that is
impeded from increasing because of restrictions on habitat, low reproductive rate, genetic segregation between
populations, low percentage of the population with breeding potential or other factors; the species is sensitive to
human activities or natural events. The polar bear is a vulnerable species in Canada as of February 2008.

Plant Index

BERRIES

(spring and summer; berries tend to occur earlier in western Canada than in eastern Canada)

Amelanchier alnifolia (saskatoonberry): late July; montane disturbed areas; up to 2 m (6½ ft) tall

Aralia nudicaulis (sarsaparilla): June and July; montane woodlands; 25 cm (10 in) tall

Arctostaphylos uva-ursi (bearberry, kinnikinick): spring and summer; montane boreal mixed woods; mat-forming; 10 cm (4 in) tall

Empetrum nigrum (crowberry): fall or overwintered spring; sphagnum hummocks, acid peatlands and coniferous/boreal forests; mat-forming; 15 cm (6 in) tall

Fragaria spp. (strawberry): spring and summer; boreal mixed woods; up to 10 cm (4 in) tall

Ribes spp. (gooseberry, currant): spring; montane moist areas; up to 1 m (3 ft) tall

Rubus spp. (raspberry, blackberry): early summer to late fall; domestic and wild; gardens, disturbed ground and boreal mixed woods; 1–2 m (3–6½ ft) tall. *R. spectabilis* (salmonberry): late summer to early fall; native to west coast; moist forests, riparian areas and coastal forests; 1–4 m (3–13 ft) tall

Sambucus spp. (elderberry): spring to late summer; montane riparian areas, open areas and forest edges; wet soils; berries in clusters; 3–4 m (10–13 ft) tall

Sheperdia canadensis (buffaloberry, soapberry, soopolallie): late July to mid-August; open woods, especially lodgepole pine forests; up to 1.5 m (5 ft) tall

Vaccinium spp. (European blueberry, bilberry, whortleberry, bog huckleberry, bog cranberry and variations of the names): summer and fall, overwintered spring; upper montane and subalpine lowlands, swampy areas, moist woods and sphagnum hummocks; damp, acidic soils; up to 15 cm (6 in) tall

Viburnum edule (highbush cranberry): late summer to early fall, overwintered spring; montane coniferous and deciduous forests, floodplains and riparian areas; moist, well-drained soils; up to 2 m (6½ ft) tall

TREES

(spring seed, late-summer and early-fall fruit and late-fall nut producers; cambium)

Betula papyrifera (birch cambium, new leaves and shoots): spring; mixed forests

Corylus americana (hazelnuts): summer and fall; eastern hardwood forests, ornamental

Crataegus spp. (hawthorns): early fall; orchards, old meadows, mixed hardwood forests, ornamental

Fagus spp. (beechnuts): fall; eastern hardwood forests

Malus spp. (apples): late summer; orchards

Pinus albicaulis (whitebark pinenuts): late summer and fall; uncommon but widely distributed within the Rockies in the subalpine; up to 10 m (33 ft) tall but stunted on windswept ridges

Populus spp. (cottonwood, aspen and poplar catkins): spring; riparian areas, mixed forests, aspen parkland

Prunus spp. (black cherry, pin cherry): summer; boreal mixed woods, orchards

Salix spp. (willow catkins): spring; riparian areas, secondary stage regrowth of disturbed sites

Sorbus aucuparia (mountain ash, rowan, dogberry): fall, overwintered spring; mixed hardwood forests, ornamental

OTHER

Carex spp. (grasses and sedges): spring to fall; open areas, disturbed sites; groundcover

Claytonia lanceolata (spring beauty): spring; montane to subalpine open areas; 10–20 cm (4–8 in) tall

Equisetum arvense (horsetail): spring to fall; moist, low-lying areas in various habitats; native to the Pacific Northwest; up to 90 cm (36 in) tall

Erythronium grandiflorum (glacier lily): spring and early summer; upper montane and subalpine; 10–40 cm (4–16 in) tall

Hedysarum spp. (hedysarum roots, bear roots, sweetvetch, Indian or Eskimo potato): May to early July; montane; up to 60 cm (24 in) tall

Heracleum lanatum (cow parsnip): summer; montane or subalpine moist areas; up to 2 m (6½ ft) tall

Oplopanax horridus (devil's club): spring and summer; montane and coastal forests; up to 3.6 m (12 ft) tall

Taraxacum spp. (dandelion): spring to early fall; disturbed ground; up to 40 cm (16 in) tall

Trifolium spp. (clover): summer; open areas and pastures; weedy species; up to 7 cm (3 in) tall

Symplocarpus foetidus / Lysichiton americanum (skunk cabbage): spring to fall; swamps or moist land; semi-aquatic, clump-forming

Valeriana officinalis (valerian): spring and summer; subalpine, ornamental aromatic; up to 40 cm (16 in) tall

**Bear grass (*Xerophyllum tenax*) is not a grass, but a lily with a corm that is not actually eaten by bears. This plant gets its name because the animal has occasionally been observed using the grass-like part of the plant as bedding in its den.

Canadian Bear Population Estimates and Documented Human Fatalities*

	Population black (BB)	Population grizzly (GB)	Population polar (PB)	Human fatalities
BC	100,000–140,000	15,000–17,000	0	** 10 BB; 3 GB (1970–2007)
AB	37,000–40,000	<500	0	** 5 BB; 7 GB (1970–2007)
SK	25,000–30,000	0	0	2 BB (1980)
MB	25,000–30,000	0	200	3 BB (1929, 1982, 2005) 2 PB (1968, 1983)
ON	75,000–100,000	0	<1,000	10 BB (1924–2007)
QC	60,000–70,000	0	Undetermined	4 BB (1983–2007)
NL/LB	6,000–10,000 (insular)	0	400–500	0
NB	16,000	0	0	0
NS	8,000–10,000	0	0	0
YK	10,000	6,000–7,000	<15,000	2 GB (1996; 2006) 2 PB (1973; 1975)
NT	5,000	800–3,000		2 BB (2001, 2005)
NU	transient	1,000–2,000		1 PB (1999)

(*) Numbers are based on the most recent data available by each provincial and territorial jurisdiction.

(**) Human fatalities in BC and Alberta are approximates owing to bear species unconfirmed in some cases or other unconfirmed or publicly unavailable data.

REFERENCES

Substantial reference material, from academic journals, government research and bear conservation organizations, in support of the information presented in this book is available online and has been compiled at www.bearscience.com.

Range maps were sourced collaboratively and cross-referentially from each of the provincial and territorial government departments of environment, wildlife and conservation. The Canadian polar bear population designations are from the IUCN/SSC Polar Bear Specialist Group.

Grizzly bear map:

Doupé, J.P., England, J.H., Furze, M. and Paetkau, D. (2007). Most northerly observation of a grizzly bear (*Ursus arctos*) in Canada: photographic and DNA evidence from Melville Island, Northwest Territories. *Arctic 80*(3), 271–276.

The following is a list of books for reference as well as recommended reading:

Davids, R.C. with Guravich, D. (1982). *Lords of the Arctic: a journey among the polar bears*. New York, NY: Macmillan Publishing Co., Inc.

Herrero, S. (2003 revised Canadian edition). *Bear Attacks: their causes and avoidances*. Toronto, ON: McClelland & Stewart Ltd.

Heur, K. (2004). *Walking the Big Wild: from Yellowstone to the Yukon on the grizzly bear's trail*. Seattle, WA: Mountaineers Books.

Hoefs, M. (ed.). (2004). *Of Man and Beast: true tales from Yukon's wilderness*. Whitehorse, YK: Amboca Ecological Services.

Lopez, B.H. (1986). *Arctic Dreams*. New York, NY: Scribner.

McClung, B. (2001). *Hiking Bear Country*. Las Vegas, NV: Life Preservers Publishing LLC.

Miles, H. and Salisbury, M. (1985). *Kingdom of the Ice Bear*. London: British Broadcasting Corporaton.

Shelton, J.G. (1994). *Bear Encounter Survival Guide*. Hagensborg, BC: Pallister Publishing.

Shelton, J.G. (2001). *Bear Attacks II: myth & reality*. Hagensborg, BC: Pallister Publishing.

Stirling, I. (1988). *Polar Bears*. Ann Arbor, MI: University of Michigan Press.

Stefansson, V. (1964). *Discovery, the autobiography of Vilhjalmur Stefansson*. Toronto, ON: McGraw Hill Book Company. See also *My Life with Eskimos* (1913) and *The Friendly Arctic* (1921).

Thayer, H. (1993). *Polar Dream*. Troutdale, OR: New Sage Press.